CAPTAIN CRASH
AND THE DALLAS
COWBOYS
FROM SIDELINE TO GOAL LINE WITH CLIFF HARRIS

CLIFF HARRIS

SP
SPORTS
PUBLISHING
L.L.C.

SportsPublishingLLC.com

ISBN-10: 1-59670-103-x
ISBN-13: 978-1-59670-103-8

Publishers: Peter L. Bannon and Joseph J. Bannon Sr.
Senior managing editor: Susan M. Moyer
Acquisitions editor: Mike Pearson
Developmental editor: Erin Linden-Levy
Art director: K. Jeffrey Higgerson
Dust jacket design: Dustin J. Hubbart
Interior layout: Dustin J. Hubbart
Imaging: Kenneth J. O'Brien

Sports Publishing L.L.C.
804 North Neil Street
Champaign, IL 61820

Phone: 1-877-424-2665
Fax: 217-363-2073
www.SportsPublishingLLC.com

Printed in the United States of America

CIP data available upon request

*This book is dedicated to those who were told they **could not** but yet they **did.***

CONTENTS

FOREWORD
by Gene Stallings

When I came to the Dallas Cowboys it was my first venture into coaching pro football. My career had taken me from a Southwest Conference championship as the head coach of Texas A&M to the Dallas Cowboys. I was hired by Tom Landry to coach the secondary.

At that time, the Cowboy defensive backs included some very savvy and talented, but aging, veterans—Mel Renfro, Cornell Green and Herb Adderly. Ultimately Herb and Mel would become members of the NFL Hall of Fame.

The secondary also included some very promising young stars in Cliff Harris, Charlie Waters, and Mark Washington. Cliff won the starting position as the Cowboys' free safety the first game of his rookie year but had to leave when he was called to active duty in the army in the middle of the season. While he was gone, Charlie replaced him and Cliff saw limited action.

The Cowboys lost in the Super Bowl to the Baltimore Colts that season. At beginning of the next year, Cliff won his spot back and the Cowboys went on to win their first Super Bowl against the Miami Dolphins. While I was a coach, there was a transition to the younger players. Herb Adderly retired, and Charlie worked his way into Herb's spot but struggled as an out-of-position cornerback. Finally, after Cornell retired, Charlie settled into his best position as strong safety. He and Cliff complemented and improved each other's play at safety. During my stint we developed the best pass defense in the NFL and won Super Bowl XII by dominating the Denver Broncos.

I enjoyed coaching Cliff because he was consumed by all aspects of the game. He made it in the pros from his small school because he studied and worked hard in practice. He forced others to match his intensity even in practice or suffer the consequences. During the games, his aggressive style of play created havoc in both the opponent's pass and run offensive schemes.

Though sometimes he was stubborn and, at times, challenged my thinking, he performed at the top of his game in the most critical situations and consistently made the big plays at pivotal times during the big games.

Cliff's love of the game and his desire to inspire others to reach for their dreams are reflected in this volume, where he describes the split personality of football—funny and painful.

I hope you enjoy reading his tales as much as I enjoyed living them!

ACKNOWLEDGMENTS

The memories recalled were worth all the effort and time dedicated to writing this book. Thanks to all of my friends who helped my recall and helped me enjoy writing about the fun from such a great era in the history of the Dallas Cowboys. Many thanks to my teammates and good friends Lee Roy Jordan, Roger Staubach, Walt Garrison, and Charlie Waters, and to the others who either recounted or wrote about their interesting experiences. Thanks also to my wife and partner, Karen, for her timely encouragement and thoughtful critique. Russ Russell, with *Dallas Cowboys Weekly,* helped me fill in some of the blank spots and allowed the use of many of the incredible photos in their archives. Thanks, also, to Cheryl Harris from the *Weekly,* for taking the time and energy to pull all the photos together for me. Thanks to Steve Richardson for the conversations that revived some old memories. And lastly, a very special thanks for the patience and effort of Erin Linden-Levy, my developmental editor, in overcoming the obstacles we faced, and without whose help the book would never have been finished.

"Nothing in the world can take the place of persistence. Talent will not; nothing is more common than unsuccessful men with talent."

—*Calvin Coolidge, 30th president of the United States (1872-1933)*

CHAPTER ONE

BEFORE I WAS A COWBOY

Becoming a Football Player

Every summer, tourists from all over the world flocked to the beautiful lakes and mountains of the resort town of Hot Springs, Arkansas. Growing up there was like living in paradise. It also created many distractions for the local high school boys, who would rather be swimming, fishing, camping or chasing girls than playing football. There was not a lot of dedication to the game, and Hot Springs High had year after year of losing records. When I was a sophomore, my young teammate buddies and I were ready for change, but we were in the minority. The older guys didn't really care. They liked the status quo.

I was dedicated to winning, but weighed in at only 150 pounds. I was too small to have much impact in games and didn't have much sway with the varsity. But our junior varsity team was undefeated that year. Even back then I enjoyed hitting hard and getting after 'em on the field.

A year later, Hot Springs hired a new coach named Ben Burton. He was determined to turn things around. Coach Burton had a new, innovative plan—get the guys in shape. He implemented a new weight program, and I began to see a difference. I started to develop confidence in my body and my ability. My athletic career and my life began to change.

I really worked hard at trying to improve my strength. Through the weight program I began to see some muscles develop, and I became one of the fastest and strongest guys on the team.

Our team was still struggling, and the coaches could have brought me up to varsity my junior year to help, but they didn't. I never got the chance, so I kept working out and getting stronger. I was about 6 feet tall and 160 pounds, and at the end of my junior year *Arkansas Football Magazine* had listed me as one of the potential stars for the Hot Springs Trojans. That got me excited, but I was a little concerned about playing for a losing team my senior year.

Then things really changed.

My dad was working for Arkansas Power and Light and was offered a promotion to become district manager. The only problem was that we had to move from Hot Springs to a small town northeast of Little Rock called Des Arc with a population of 1,487.

My dad didn't force me to move to Des Arc. He asked me to come with him and spend some time there in the summer before my senior year. He wanted me to check it out and then make my decision. To make my decision tougher, one of my high school coaches in Hot Springs told me I could stay with him and his wife in the downstairs portion of their house on Lake Hamilton when my family moved to Des Arc. I was torn.

My dad and I visited Des Arc and talked with John Rollins, the head football coach, and some of his assistants. They told us they really wanted me to play for them. They had all the positions filled

As Des Arc's quarterback, I led the team to an undefeated season my senior year, 1966. *Photo courtesy of Cliff Harris*

The 1966 Des Arc High School football team—I'm No. 10.
Photo courtesy of Cliff Harris

except for quarterback, which was my position, and they had the potential to be a good team.

Some of the cheerleaders drove me around the town and showed me the sights—the flat farming terrain, the White River, and the soybean, rice, and cotton fields around the area. This certainly was not like the mountains where I grew up, but I sure liked the interest the coaches and the cheerleaders had shown in me. There was also the potential to win.

I decided to move to Des Arc with my family, and it was the best thing that could have happened to me. I quarterbacked an undefeated team and was on my way to playing more football. After my senior year, Ouachita Baptist University offered me a full scholarship. My future in football was beginning to unfold.

Almost a Hog

In the fall when leaves changed to a fiery bright red, so did the passion in the hearts of all the sports fans in Arkansas. The autumn chill in the air meant two things: hunting and Razorbacks football. Razorbacks footballers were legends to Arkansas kids of any age who ever wore shoulder pads and a helmet. From when I was a kid until even today, there has been no team in all of sports that sparked the interest of Arkansas sports fans like the Hogs.

Even though my dad attended Ouachita Baptist University for his undergraduate degree—he later went to U of A for his master's— and my mom Henderson Methodist College in Arkadelphia, Arkansas, they both followed the Razorbacks.

My maternal grandfather, Ansel Weaver, was the most avid Razorbacks fan in our family. He lived in the small mountain town of Glenwood, Arkansas, and loved football. His excitement and passion drove my initial interest in the game. My grandmother, Amy, was a math teacher named "Teacher of the Century" in the small town for her devotion and commitment to her students and teaching.

Ansel and Amy never missed a Razorbacks home game, which was played at Fayetteville or Little Rock. They went to the game with another couple from Glenwood and sometimes took me with them to the afternoon games. We all put something red on, packed a lunch, and went up Highway 71, the winding mountain road to the University of Arkansas through the beautiful Ozark Mountains. It was a breathtaking ride through the forests, although it was a narrow, curvy, and dangerous two-lane road. The car was filled with excitement, but I usually got carsick on the way. I recovered enough by game time. Hearing the deafening "Piggg Sooeeeyyyy!" echoing through valley somehow brought me around.

I was the first athlete from Ouachita Baptist University to go pro.
Photo courtesy of Cliff Harris

When the Hogs played home games in Little Rock, they practiced in Hot Springs on the same field where I practiced. My football buddies and I went down to the field we had vacated to sit in the stands and watch them go through their short pregame practice. I knew all of the players, but they did not know me.

Those moments fueled my fire. While in the stands, I could imagine myself someday wearing the red helmet with a hog emblem on the side. I didn't ultimately play for the Hogs, and today I am very proud of the fact that I followed my father's footsteps to Ouachita Baptist University and became the first professional athlete to graduate from there. Football also became a family tradition that has been carried on through the years. My younger brother, Tommy, played for Arkansas. I have three sons that play football—at the University of Richmond, one at Arkansas, and another at Rockwell High School. Some of my greatest joys in life are watching them play. Thanks to Ansel, those early trips to the games were the beginning of many years of my love for the game of football.

Shin Shame

The general public seems to think that any college football player can pick a pro football team and just show up at the team's training camp and try out as a free agent. That is not even close to reality.

I was the only player from Ouachita who was invited to try out for an NFL team that year and one of the few in the state. Such was the case for most of the small colleges in Arkansas, Texas, and all over the U.S.—then and now. The larger colleges even have very few players who get a shot at the big leagues. But there are more opportunities today thanks to the indoor Arena Football League and the NFL Europe League.

During my junior year, the scouts started showing up at OBU and running me through different types of tests. This awakened my interest to the possibility of playing pro football. If I had truly known the odds, I would have probably studied harder in class. Like most young folks, though, I had big dreams. I could see myself tearing up the receivers in the pros just as I did in the NAIA. All I could do was give it a shot and give it my all if I was given the chance.

One spring day a scout passed through Arkadelphia. These guys were generally cocky, because very few, if any, people involved with pro football teams reached out to the small college communities very much. When the scouts came to town there was an air of curiosity on the campus and they were treated almost like celebrities. Some were good guys, but all were cocky.

I was ready for any of their tests, because I was in excellent condition. I had been running track for Ouachita all season. It was close to our conference meet, and I was peaking at just the right time. I felt good about my 440 times and felt I had a chance to place in the meet.

Besides running, one test I was asked to perform was a standing jump. You started with both feet on the ground then exploded straight up. When you reached the apex, you marked a spot on the wall with the blue chalk that was on your fingertips. The test, of course, measured leaping ability, but it also quantified explosiveness. I jumped 39 inches, which impressed the scout. But I wasn't sure how that stacked up against other recruits.

Back at the dorm, all of my buddies wanted to know about every aspect of my meeting with the big-time guys and how I did. They wanted to know all about the tests. The next morning before classes, the chatter was still going on the grounds outside our "jock" dorm, which housed all the football players.

Around the dorm entrance there was a covered, concrete patio area that had a couple of iron chairs for lounging around.

Surrounding the patio was a brick wall. Some of my teammates and other students were standing around BS-ing before the chimes rang and sent everyone scrambling across the "ravine" to their classes.

The topic of discussion continued to be my testing. Of course, no one believed any of the results, thinking they were exaggerated. I described my standing jump, but everyone questioned the height. One of the guys pointed at the brick wall around the patio and declared it was about 39 inches tall.

I told them, "Okay, I'll prove I can jump that high. I'll jump flat-footed to the top of the wall." I thought that would finally shut everyone up. I knew I could do it.

Everyone gathered around and got quiet. At the time, I had on a pair of tight, white Levis. They were the newest fad. I did not calculate their tightness or care. I thought adrenaline would work for me and carry me over the top.

I toed the wall and focused. I bent my knees and, with a grunt, exploded upward with all my might. I felt myself flying toward the top of the wall. My toes found the front edge, but that was it. My momentum did not carry me completely to the top where I could land safely. My toes hit, then instantly slipped backwards. On my way back down, my right shin smacked the edge and excruciating pain shot up my leg. I fell backward, but managed to land on my feet. All the guys standing around began to chuckle and told me I didn't make it.

When the crowd dispersed, I bent over to rub my wounded shin. About that time a little red began to show through, then ultimately cover, the leg of my new white Levis. I could feel a dent in my shin, so I pulled my pants leg up. There was an inch-and-a-half-long gash across the top of my shin. Damn! Bad timing! It hurt like the devil, but I was not about to show any pain to anyone. My roommate, Jim Boyette, grabbed my arm and said,

"Let's go to the infirmary to get that looked at." We jumped in his car and took off.

We were driving through the ravine when the head track coach, Bob Gravette, was coming from the opposite direction in his VW. He spotted us and flagged us down. I was in the passenger's side front seat holding my shin when he proudly held up a brand new pair of track shoes. He said, "Cliff, look what I have for you— new Tokyos! (The best track shoe at the time.) You have been doing so well, I wanted to make sure that you have a chance to run your best time in the conference meet."

I couldn't think of anything to say except, "Great! Thanks, Coach!"

I made it to the infirmary and got eight stitches in my leg. I ran in the conference meet a few days later in my new shoes, stitches and all. I did not set any records that day, but I did learn a valuable lesson: I didn't have to prove anything to anyone but myself ever again.

Disappointment

Life was going on as usual at Ouachita Baptist University. Kids were busily scampering into their classes. They were studying for tests, doing homework, or just lazily chatting up their friends. It was a typical cold spring day in Arkadelphia.

But not for me. It was NFL draft day. And I was on cloud nine.

All morning as I attended my classes, my mind was somewhere else. I kept repeating the words that Cowboys director of player personnel Gil Brandt had told me over and over again in my mind.

"Cliff, we're going to draft you in the first six rounds."

I was going to be a Dallas Cowboy. I couldn't wait for the draft to start.

After class I went by the "jock" dorm to see if any of the guys had found it on TV. There were only three stations on the set in the first floor social area, and none of them was carrying the draft. There was no ESPN, no all-sports networks, no sports talk radio. Only real sports buffs knew the draft was going on—and even then trying to find out what had happened was impossible.

But I wasn't going to let that bring me down. I did the only thing I knew to do, which was go back to my off-campus apartment and wait for the call. A couple of my teammates came with me to share in the excitement. All we had to do was wait for the phone to ring.

And it did.

"This is it!" I thought as I grabbed the receiver.

"Have they called yet?" asked one of my pals who could not restrain himself on the other end of the line.

"No!" I replied abruptly. "I will let you know as soon as I hear anything!"

A little while later the phone clanged again and I pounced on it. But time and again, it was just friends checking in.

The more the phone rang, the more disappointment I felt with every hang up. I recalled how I had thought Brandt's promise of the first six rounds was too good to be true, but he had convinced me he was serious, and I had believed him. Now I felt some doubt creeping back in. I remembered how I had been overlooked in college, and that began to weigh on my mind. Maybe the NFL wouldn't really happen for me, just a skinny kid from Arkadelphia.

The afternoon went on, and no call from the Cowboys came. When day one of the draft was over, I was alone in my apartment and so down.

"They've gone through the first eight rounds—so much for being in the first six," I huffed. "Well, there is still half of the draft left. Maybe Mr. Brandt will call tomorrow in the later rounds. That would be okay."

The next day came and went. No call. The clock struck midnight, and I knew the draft was over and I assumed so were my chances with the Cowboys.

"Br-r-r-ing," the phone's ring pierced the silent apartment.

"Hello?" I answered.

"Cliff?" the voice asked. "This is Gil Brandt. Look, we had some complications during the draft, but we are still interested. We want to sign you to a free agent contract. I have someone I am sending your way tomorrow with a contract. All you have to do is sign it."

I listened but was upset about the broken promise, and the contract offer did not console me. Throughout my whole life I had always had to prove myself on the field in high school and in college, and now that looked to be the case in the NFL. If the Cowboys didn't want me enough to draft me, I would prove myself some other way.

"Look," I explained, "don't send anyone here. I am not going to sign."

Brandt tried to change my mind, but I was too disappointed to listen. I hung up the phone, thinking about the other teams who had shown some interest, and I tried to bury the idea of me in a Cowboys uniform.

The next morning I decided to go visit my mentor and inspiration, Coach Benson and see what he thought I should do. I knew he knew I hadn't been drafted, but he acted like he had not heard. I told him what had happened and how disappointed I was. He sat back and mulled over the options.

"Cliff," he said in his normal confident tone, "I really think you should reconsider what they offered. They have shown the most interest in you."

My college coach, Buddy Bob Benson, watches over my shoulder as I sign my first contract with the Dallas Cowboys.
Photo courtesy of Special Collections, Ouachita Baptist University, Arkadelphia, Arkansas

As I headed back to my apartment I thought about what Coach Benson said. A few hours later Brandt called me back, and I decided to follow my friend's advice.

"Mr. Brandt, I have changed my mind," I said. "Go ahead and send your guy up here."

The next day the Cowboys representative arrived in Arkadelphia and offered me a three-year contract with a $500 bonus.

I took $100 of the bonus and bought a new stereo. I was on my way.

CHAPTER TWO

LIFE AS A ROOKIE

Steaks for Every Meal

I t was official: I was a Dallas Cowboy. Now I just had to get myself ready for training camp, which I knew would be both a challenge and an opportunity to really show what I was made of. I wanted to be in tip-top shape.

With the Cowboys workout manual in hand, I built my own bench press and kept it in the garage where I parked my car. I borrowed one of OBU's bars and used flywheels for the weights. It worked, and I really made good use of it.

The Cowboys put me on an 8,000-calorie-per-day diet to help me gain weight. All I did was eat and work out. I ate steaks for breakfast and dinner, finishing each meal with two cans of food supplement. I was driven to be in the best possible shape. I ate, ran, lifted, rested, and then repeated the process all day long. I tried to get some of my former Ouachita football teammates to work out with me, but it was their off-season and they wanted to enjoy it. So I worked out mainly by myself. At the beginning of the program, I weighed about 184; after three months I had gained about six pounds. After weeks of running and weight training I was ready for camp.

On July 10, 1970 I left Little Rock's airport. Destination: Thousand Oaks, California, where the Cowboys held their training camp at California Lutheran College—a quiet place (until we arrived) near Los Angeles, about 20 miles from Malibu Beach. I studied my playbook all the way to L.A. I followed a big guy off the plane into the mass of people at the L.A. airport. I thought, by some outside chance, he might be a Cowboy rookie. So I asked him if he was heading to T.O. He just pointed and said, "Yes. Follow me this way."

He said, "Call me 'Ropes,'" because he knew the ropes. His real name, I found out, was Pat Toomay. He was a Vanderbilt grad whose dad was a general in the air force. He had lived in California before and felt right at home. I didn't.

I did follow him, and we were off to a great adventure. Pat made the team as a defensive end and was my roommate for many years.

Meeting Charlie

After I signed the free-agent contract, I was invited to visit Dallas along with a few other select rookies who were drafted. The Cowboys' front office was evaluating their new crop—running us through some tests—and gave us a workout manual. That trip is where I first met Charlie Waters.

Charlie was drafted in the third round but did not seem very excited. He told me he was uncomfortable with the Cowboys' plan for him. He had played both quarterback and wide receiver in college, but the Cowboys were planning to move him to defensive back. I knew ultimately he might be my competition for a spot on the team, but for the moment I just enjoyed his company.

We had a rural, middle-class upbringing in common and hit it off immediately. After a long day of being tested and scrutinized, the Cowboys took us back to out hotel, and Charlie and I decided to check out the big city and hit a few of the Dallas nightspots.

I never expected that we would ultimately find ourselves so closely intertwined and working together—depending on each other for success. We became an integral part of the Cowboys' "Doomsday Defense" and were an unbeatable tandem at free safety and strong safety. After our run, we retired from long football careers that truly maximized and complemented each other's talent. In fact, we are such a good team that we work together even now in the energy business.

The Vets Are Coming

One of the reasons I made the Cowboys was because the 1970 training camp lasted longer than normal and the coaches had more time to watch me perform. The National Football League Players Association (NFLPA) was on strike, and the veterans came to camp six weeks late. The Cowboys planned ahead and, in expectation of a long camp, brought in more than their usual number of rookies. There were 120 young warriors vying for a chance at stardom with the Dallas Cowboys. We were all staying at empty summer dorms at California Lutheran College, better known as CLC.

The two practices a day were hard, long, and intense. That, combined with the meeting that started right after dinner and lasted until 10 p.m., meant we were exhausted.

After the first week, guys were being sent home daily. Line coach Jim Myers called a name and told the guy to take his playbook to Coach Landry. I think Jim liked that part of his job. Of course, that meant the "Turk" was visiting, and someone was going to get the ax. Cut. Sent home.

Us rookies watched in awe as the vets filed off the bus at training camp.
Photo courtesy of www.CowboysWeekly.com

After a few weeks of busting tail and a few rookie games, guys could see how they stacked up against the other rookie competitors. Some knew that with the vets not even there yet, the writing was on the wall, and they wanted to go home. They visited Coach Landry on their own. Sometimes the Cowboys—even though they knew some of the players did not have a chance to make the team—kept the men, because if those guys left, the practice lines would be too short and everyone would be exhausted. They refused to give the players tickets home. That didn't always stop a guy, though. I heard that some hitch-hiked home.

After several weeks of practice, the rookies had been thinned down some, and the ones remaining had definitely been toughened up. Coming from Ouachita, which is a National Association of Intercollegiate Athletics (NAIA) team, I did not know what to expect from my rookie competition in the Cowboys training camp. The majority of players came from the big leagues—NCAA Division I-A schools. I did find out quickly that I could compete with them and I could knock them out if needed. I discovered they were not really that much bigger or faster than the players I had competed against in college. I also found out that my hit could take any of them out.

Now, though, the rubber was about to meet the road, because the strike had ended and the vets were coming to town. None of us rooks knew what to expect. Were these guys going to be giants? Were they all going to be unbelievably better than us? After all, these guys were playing in the NFL. We had been watching them on television for years. Now we were going to meet them face to face and literally head on.

"I am going to get into my zone and bring it," I thought as I tried to pump myself up. "I am going to go as hard as I can and give it all that I can, because that is all I can do. If it works, it works. If it doesn't, I gave it all I had and had a good time doing it."

I was still very nervous.

When the stars began to arrive at CLC, most drove their own rented cars so they would have a way to get around while in camp. They began to pour in one afternoon after our practice. All of the rooks were in their rooms, which overlooked the CLC parking lot where the vets were arriving. As they got out of their cars, we all gathered in the rooms where we could watch and see if we could pick out the big-name players.

"There's Craig Morton!"

"Wow, there's Lance Rentzel."

"There's Ralph Neely. Man, is he big."

Then there were those we did not recognize and were guessing who they might be. I kept my eyes open for Mel Renfro, the great All-Pro Cowboys defensive back.

Morton and Rentzel drove up together in a convertible. With them, we noticed astounded, was Rentzel's wife, TV actress Joey Heatherton. Heatherton was a blond bombshell, and all of the guys were falling out of the windows over her as Morton hoisted Joey onto his shoulders and carried her through the parking lot.

"Gosh, man, this is the big time now!" I thought as we watched the superstars kid around.

I knew where I stood with the rooks surrounding me at that window, but I did not know how I would stack up against the vets. I was going to find out very soon—and so were they!

Bob Hayes—Trial by Fire

The first day of practice with the veterans was a tense situation for the rooks, but the vets seemed to be loose and happy just to be back in the game after the strike. Every player was under constant scrutiny and analysis. All of the practices were filmed from the tower, an erected 30-foot lookout above the practice field. Coach Tom Landry peered down over his domain much of the time during practice. The film from the tower was then reviewed first by the coaches and then the players. Coaches with clipboards were everywhere, making detailed notes on individual performances.

The practice started with the whole team doing traditional warmup exercises like side-the-straddle hop before we broke down into specific position groups. Coach Bobby Franklin and then later coach Gene Stallings led the defensive backs. We concentrated on stretching and worked on flexibility, which helped me stay healthy throughout my career.

After we loosened up and went through some running and coverage-type drills, we went into man-to-man coverage. I started my career as a cornerback and later was moved to free safety. But I

The first day the vets were at camp, I had to cover Bob Hayes (22), who was, at that time, "The World's Fastest Man."

really liked corner because I felt it was the ultimate physically challenging position in the NFL. The guys who play that lonely, pressure-filled position have the toughest job in the game. I had been covering the rookies and doing a good job against them thus far in camp. Now was the real test—the vets.

The way the drill worked was the receivers got in a line and the defensive backs lined up across from them off of the field. When it was his turn, the receiver went over and talked to the quarterback to discuss what route he wanted to run against the weary cornerback, who took his position on the field and waited for the conference to end. When the call had been made, the receiver lined up opposite the defender and both waited for the ball to be snapped.

It was pure man-to-man coverage with no help from any linebackers or safeties. It was all up to you. While you were in line waiting for your turn, you could count back and find out who you would be covering.

The first day after the vets arrived, I did not like what I found when I counted back to see whom I was paired with.

Bob Hayes.

Bob was a very loose guy, always laughing and cutting up. He did not appear to be too intense.

I was. Intense and nervous.

I was about to cover "The World's Fastest Man," the title he received when he won and tied the current world record in the 100-meter dash in the 1964 Tokyo Olympics.

Back home watching television in Arkadelphia, I had seen him blow by NFL defensive backs like they were standing still. And now the skinny kid from OBU was about to be tested against him.

Suddenly it was our turn. As we got ready, I felt my stomach tighten with nerves, and I felt sick. But I did not show it. I kept my cool.

Bob went over to Craig Morton, the quarterback, and they looked over at me, then called a route.

"Is he going to try to blow by me for a take off? Is it a sideline or a curl?" I thought as I got mentally ready. "I will take a chance and jump him early and take away all his short routes. That way if it is a streak, I will do my best to run with him."

The ball was snapped, and Bob blazed off faster than I had ever seen before. He closed the space between us, and I backpedaled as fast as I could. Then I slowed to break with him.

I was focused on all of his running movement and actions. When his head dipped and he slowed down, I felt I had guessed correctly. He was running a 15-yard deep turn in.

When he slowed to make his break, I stopped my backpedal and broke toward him. I saw that Craig had released the ball as I headed toward Hayes. Just as the ball reached Bob's hands, I reached over and hit it away without touching Bob.

All of the young defensive backs cheered.

I had covered my first NFL receiver, one of the best who had ever played, a player who changed the game of football and deserves to be in the Hall of Fame.

"Good job, rookie," Bob said unfazed and trotted back to the offensive side.

I did not say anything at all, just jogged back to my fellow defensive backs. I did not want to act cocky—yet.

I felt pretty good. I had passed my first test, and it had been a good one.

I was back in line and with about three defensive backs ahead of me when Hayes got back to the front of the line. He and Craig had already called a play and he was jogging into position when he looked at me and smiled as he motioned for me to cut in front of the other prospects and come line up against him.

I gulped and moved into position to cover him. I did not know what to expect, but I knew that "Speedo" wanted to redeem himself so I lined up a step deeper than normal.

The ball was snapped, and he took off toward me. He approached the transitional area where I had to be ready to move one way or the other, the spot where a defensive back tests his goods.

Bob faked a quick break outside. I slowed for just an instant with that move, and that was when he took off.

I had never seen acceleration like that on the fields at OBU. As Bob blew by me, I heard him chuckle as he went by. He was having some fun at my expense.

I chased after him and closed the distance as best as I could, but Craig lobbed the ball over my head and Bob made the easy grab that would have been a touchdown.

I had just been beaten by the best.

As Bob jogged back by me, he smiled and said, "Welcome to the NFL, rookie."

I always remembered that line.

Making the Cut

Every day of training camp, my roommate Pat Toomay, my good buddy Charlie Waters, and I took the list of rookies and tried to figure out who would be cut. We were perfectly qualified to sleuth because, based on our positions, we covered the spectrum of the team. As a defensive lineman, Pat came in contact with his fellow linemen, the offensive linemen, and the running backs; Charlie and I checked out the other defensive backs, the linebackers, and the receivers.

That day—one of the final cut days where the roster went from 120 rookies to 20—we poured over the list. Pat and I had to cut six guys to make it down to the final number, and we were on No. 5

when we looked at the names left of the list and then at each other. We both looked at Charlie.

"Hey, sorry Charlie," I said. "You're the guy."

A few hours later, the Cowboys let him go. Fortunately for all of us, they brought him back not long after.

The whittling-down process got in our heads during games.

I was playing free safety in a late preseason game against the Oilers in the Astrodome. It was getting very, very competitive—even downright cutthroat.

We were in a formation where I was to cover the outside third of the field instead of the middle of the field, which was a free safety's standard coverage area. Lining up with me was a guy who was competing for my position. The ball was snapped and the Oilers threw a deep pass down the middle into my competitor's territory. Normally I follow my strengths and try to cover a lot of ground, more than just my specific zone, but when I saw this guy getting beat, I stayed in my spot.

I could have come over and made the play. But I didn't.

The receiver caught the pass for a touchdown.

The Cowboys cut the guy the next day. It was one less player in the competition that Charlie or I had to deal with.

In the end, all three of us—Pat, Charlie, and I—beat out the final cut. But it was good rookie fun to speculate who might make it and who might not. Plus, it kept us sharp and made us aware of the competition.

Low-Key Landry

I would never have been able to play a single day of pro football if I had not believed in myself. As is also true in life, to maximize performance in any sport, an athlete must first be prepared in his mind. Mental acuity transcends physical prowess. It was this creed upon which I built my future in professional athletics. I was not a physical phenom like many of my competitors. I won through preparation, wits, and an indescribable mental edge. But I had to make changes in how I motivated myself when I made it to the NFL.

As in life, young people are easily molded and directed. In college my coach, Buddy Bob Benson, always delivered an energized speech prior to each game that moved me into a zone.

"To win today we need maximum performance levels and to leave all you have on the field because that is what it will take to beat these guys. We are not very talented, but we have worked harder than anyone else, and I've made you tougher than any of those guys you will line up against out there today!" From the depths of his soul, he convincingly appealed to us.

As he rallied us around him, I felt a controlled intensity building and burning inside of me. He would tell us, "If you think you are beaten, you are. If you want to win, but don't think you can, you won't." As trite as it might sound, those words before my college games fueled my fire. Bursting with thoughts of victory and glory, we hit the field with intensity.

I remembered those moments as I stood in the dressing room of San Diego Stadium before my first professional football game, a preseason contest against the Chargers, and anxiously awaited the pregame pep talk from coach Tom Landry. I had already gone through my pregame routine of ankle-taping and sitting quietly, going over the game plan one more time.

I had been named the starting right cornerback for the Dallas Cowboys. After many long weeks of training camp, it was time for the *real* test.

"Well, at least I can go back to Arkansas and show everybody that I had played for the Cowboys," I thought as I put on my pads for the first professional football game I had seen live. "I am starting at right corner for the Dallas Cowboys. Wow!"

Coach Landry inspired us in strange and often quiet ways. He wasn't much for sideline antics or locker-room displays. *Photo courtesy of www.CowboysWeekly.com*

I was pumped up and mentally ready to be motivated by Coach Landry. I expected similar inspiration as I had received from Coach Benson just a year before at Ouachita Baptist.

"If Coach Benson was so good at it, imagine what Coach Landry will be like with all of his experience in the professional ranks!" I eagerly thought as I finished getting ready.

I made sure I was the first one dressed, and I took a seat in the front row directly in front of the podium where the great Tom Landry was to deliver his pregame remarks. As the guys gradually filtered into the room and sat down around me, I was all ready to be inspired.

The younger guys prepared quickly; the veterans were saving their energy and taking their time. It seemed like an eternity before Landry stoically approached the podium. I felt the energy in the air and the rumbling turning quiet.

As Coach Landry got ready to speak, no one said anything. He looked out at us and began to speak.

"We had a very good training camp, and today will be the first step toward the Super Bowl," he stated very deliberately in his normal tone.

I believed him.

He then talked about the offensive game plan and a few specific plays. Then he went over our defensive priorities—stop the running game and some other keys. He mentioned a few of the Chargers' offensive tendencies.

"Now, it is time to go out and execute," he said matter-of-factly and left the podium.

I watched in disbelief as he walked away. I was not ready for him to leave. I needed more inspiration. I sat there, thinking he might come back, as most of the players started down the hall to the tunnel that led to the field. I watched them file out.

"I don't have any option," I thought in disappointment. "I better get going."

I said a prayer and hit the tunnel. When I ran out onto the field, I looked around at the thousands of cheering fans. I immediately felt the change as I stared at the crowd. It was the beginning of my life in pro football. I knew Ouachita was behind me.

"Today it is up to me. So this is what it is all about. I have just gone from a boy to a man," I thought as I made my way to the sideline. "From an amateur to a pro. If it is to be, it is up to me."

That was the beginning of my cold river philosophy of life. When you are standing on the bank of a rushing, cold river with a bear coming down the mountain to eat you, you have two options: Number one—you can stand there and be eaten by the bear, or number two—jump into the river and swim like hell!

Life is like that cold river. You really do not have an option. Dive in and swim like hell to the other side—and never look back!

Toppling the Giants

The tempo was definitely different for my first regular-season game in Dallas in September 1970, which was nationally televised. The vets were serious and focused after beating Philadelphia in the season opener out East.

I was, too. I was the starting free safety for the Dallas Cowboys.

You could feel the intensity in the air. The pressure was on. The veteran players knew coach Tom Landry was not showing the stress he was feeling after years of disappointment and the team being labeled as "Next Year's Champion." He and the rest of the team wanted to change that this year.

We were playing the New York Giants, a team Coach Landry had both played for and coached, and the game was important to him personally. He told us if we wanted to make All-Pro we should play well against New York, because it was the media capital of the world. I listened to him. (The message hit home with me. About half of the game balls I received during my career came from games against the Giants. I liked to play them.)

Before the game began, both teams lined up side by side about 10 yards apart in the tunnel, a tradition that was unique to the Cotton Bowl, where the home and visiting teams entered and left the field through the same entrance.

I was nervous as a cat. Right there beside me was the enemy.

I tried to sneak looks at them without them noticing. Here were the guys I had watched on television while laying on the couch at my girlfriend's parents' house back in Arkadelphia.

I looked over and saw the great Giants quarterback, a scrambler, and an intense competitor, Fran Tarkenton. He was calm and even laughing as he chatted with his teammates.

"Wow," I thought, "he is laughing and I am about to throw up."

Then I saw No. 43, Spider Lockhart, the Giants' great free safety. He was a guy I really admired. I thought he could really play.

Discreetly, I looked further to size up a threat of mine, Clifton McNeil from Grambling State—a tall and skinny world-class sprinter.

"I am going to knock you out today, and you don't even know it!" I thought as I looked him up and down.

We ran onto the field before the screaming fans. Even though the atmosphere was very different than Ouachita, it felt the same to me; I was in the zone and did not hear anything.

I was ready.

We did not play very well in the first half. We were behind 10-0. Both teams went up the tunnel quietly, and we went to our separate dressing rooms. After things settled down Coach Landry called us all together. I had never seen him this upset. He began to tell us how important this game was, how poorly we were playing against one of our Eastern Division rivals, and how embarrassed he was.

My great day against the Giants included this interception, which led to a touchdown. *Photo courtesy of www.CowboysWeekly.com*

"You all are not playing like professionals but like amateurs just drawing pay," he said.

"Wow, I can't believe what I am seeing or hearing," I thought as he continued to show major emotion and feeling.

It hit me and inspired me just like my OBU coach Buddy Bob Benson used to do during our halftimes.

In the first series of the second half, the Giants had the ball in their own territory when Tarkenton unleashed a bomb to one of his speedy receivers. I read him, broke on the ball, and took it away from the receiver, who tried to tackle me, but I shook him off and started weaving toward our goal line. After breaking a few tackles I was dragged down at about the 5-yard line. From there our offense had no trouble pushing it in for a touchdown. We moved to within three points, 10-7.

We kicked off to the Giants and they started their drive on their 20-yard line. Fran then gave me another gift that I picked off and ran back to the Dallas 40. Our offense was not on track and missed a field goal.

I was having a good day. My good day continued with a fumble recovery on the Giants' next drive, which led to the go-ahead touchdown, 14-10. We ended up beating the Giants 28-10.

Landry was happy and so was I. My performance in the game assured me my position and a place on the Cowboys roster. Thank you, Fran.

Golly

After the Giants game I was asked to be interviewed for the television program and comment on the game. The control room was off to the side of the tunnel. When I entered the tiny room, it was full of activity. People were scurrying everywhere around the camera and the light stands. The lights were glaring.

Then I saw one of my favorite players, Frank Gifford, in a coat and tie and he was sitting very calmly on a stool in front of a camera.

"Go on over there, Cliff," someone told me.

I walked over to him.

"Golly, Mister Gifford. I have always wanted to meet you!" I exclaimed, not knowing he was on the air.

My statement caught him completely off guard.

"Cliff, you had quite a game," he stammered. "Could you tell us about the first interception?"

Once I heard the question, I realized the camera was on and the television audience was watching. It was my turn to be caught off guard.

I did the best a country boy could do for his first time on national television. The headline in the *Dallas Morning News* the next day read, "Golly, Mister Gifford." Folks in Arkansas loved my golly statement and still tease me about it even today. Because this was the season we won our first Super Bowl, our public relations department put together the year's highlight film. In it they recounted how our offense came from behind to resoundingly win the game. What a welcome to the NFL!

You're in the Army Now!

At the height of the Vietnam War in 1970, I joined the U.S. National Guard. I played in the Cowboys' first five regular-season games and was the Oakfarms MVP in two of those. The fifth game was a 54-13 loss to Minnesota. I was not in a good mood the next morning as I flew to Fort Polk, Louisiana, for basic training. I was having a great year so far and didn't want to stop playing.

When we arrived at Fort Polk they gave us all our gear in green bags. We stepped off the buses and stood there between the barracks for an hour, then sat on our bags for another two hours. Then it started to pour. We didn't have any rain gear on. It rained so hard, little rivers formed.

Finally, they herded us into a room, where they made us count off and get into lines. They had to inoculate everyone in preparation for going overseas to Vietnam—several shots. We walked in a line with our shirts off—a straight line—with 50-100 guys. And they had these vaccination guns and they would put them up to your arm and they would go pap-pap, pap-pap. Instead of needles, it was air that forced the vaccine into the arm. A guy in front of me passed out and fell to the floor as soon as they zapped him.

Then we all lined up for haircuts. At the time, everybody's hair was real long, even the Cowboys players. We all had long sideburns. Charlie Waters looked like Prince Valiant. When I look back at the pictures, I notice Coach Landry even had long hair and long sideburns. We got buzz haircuts in the army.

We were isolated from the world during basic training. Everybody wanted to call home, but we had to wait in line to use the phone on the post. There were maybe 20 guys in line to call home, and we each got two minutes to talk.

At the very beginning they would not let the new recruits out of the platoon area. Then a week later, they wouldn't let us leave the company area. Then the next week, we were allowed to go to the PX. We could never leave Fort Polk during basic training. At first we couldn't watch television, either. But finally we were allowed to watch it.

One cold, rainy day a lot of the guys on the base were watching the Cowboys play the New York Giants at Yankee Stadium. I didn't watch the game at all. I couldn't watch it. I was supposed to be there.

I missed the Kansas City and Philadelphia games, too. They let me leave the base, finally, and I returned to the team the night the Cowboys played the St. Louis Cardinals, a 38-0 loss, televised on *Monday Night Football*.

After that, on Friday nights, I flew out of Fort Polk to Dallas. And the next day I was on my way to either St. Louis or New York or Detroit. Then I returned to the base after the game.

The rest of my platoon was stuck on the base, so when I would get back, I would tell them what was going on and how life was on the outside. They were happy about that and they were happy they could watch me on Sundays when the Cowboys played.

New York Sausage

Because I was a platoon leader in the army, I met guys who came from all over the country. I was surprised to find most of these young men were in their teens. It was certainly easier for the army to mold young minds. They were from all over, but most were from the South and a spattering was from Arkansas, Texas, and Louisiana. There were also a few from back East.

Victor Mastrovincinzo was a short, pudgy, but energetic Italian from the Big Apple. He was very likeable and friendly, and we really got along. He was a very intense and committed fan of the Yankees and the Giants.

The year after my stint in the army, the Cowboys played at Yankee Stadium. It was one of those unbelievable moments. Wow, I was about to play a game in the famous Yankee Stadium, which I had only seen on TV. When we were in the dressing room to suit up before the game, I remembered the names of the great players who played for the Yankees, Joe DiMaggio, Mickey Mantle, and Babe Ruth. Just think of all the people who had played there, and now I was about to go onto that same field where those legends had played to perform myself. I was overwhelmed.

"This is a one-time experience," I thought as I took it all in. "Who knows if I will make it back here? I am going to stick around as long as I can and enjoy every minute of it. Then I can at least say I was in Yankee Stadium—even if I get cut before the next game."

Also used as a baseball field, it was an interesting place to play because the fans were right down on the field and very close to the opposing players bench. When you stood up behind the bench, the fans could reach out and touch you. There was some razzing going on from the avid fans because the Giants were keeping the game close early. In the third quarter amidst the catcalls, I was sitting on the bench and I heard my name called from the stands by a voice I recognized. I turned around and looked. It was my old friend from Fort Polk who had come down out of the stands to the fence between the crowd and the sidelines. He was smiling his big smile, and I wanted to go over and talk to him, but because I was a new guy, I looked around first to see if any of the coaches were watching. They were all focused on the field, so I snuck back. When I went over to him, he handed me a cylindrical package.

"It is a homemade Italian sausage," he said.

"Thanks," I replied.

"I am glad to see you here," he said with a smile.

He had remembered how I had suffered last season when I was stuck with him at Fort Polk in basic training and had missed my chance to play the Giants in Yankee Stadium. He knew how badly I had wanted to be out on the playing field then.

We visited for a few more minutes before I had to get back to the game.

After he left, I handed the sausage to an equipment man for safekeeping. He stored it somewhere until we got back on the plane to return to Dallas after our 42-14 win. After takeoff, the equipment man and I had a little victory meal—Victor Mastrovincinzo's Italian sausage.

CHAPTER THREE

THE COWBOY WAY

Landry Mile

For a pro football player to perform at high levels consistently means a broad spectrum of top physical conditioning. In the early years of pro football, the players came to training camp out of shape then worked out hard in camp along with preseason games and got themselves into shape in summer before the football season began, hence the term "training camp."

As in typical Coach Landry style, he always looked for an edge. One of the last areas to be addressed by most teams in the NFL was endurance. Landry thought if you came into camp in shape, you would have more time to perfect your skills like running plays or catching passes versus just running wind sprints. Since football is a sprinting game, most of the early players placed very little, if any, focus on long-term endurance. Coach Landry bounced on the edge and derived his theory of aerobic conditioning for football from the world-famous Dr. Ken Cooper

Training camp at Thousand Oaks included a conditioning test, known fondly as the "Landry Mile." *Photo courtesy of www.CowboysWeekly.com*

from the Cooper Clinic in Dallas. Dr Cooper was known worldwide for expertise in the study of human-conditioning levels and related heart studies. It all meshed together.

In Landry's eyes, to be in top condition meant training vigorously in all areas. When we arrived in camp, before any pads were put on, Landry would welcome us to Thousand Oaks by administering his test called the "Landry Mile." It was a 12-minute "aerobic" test to determine if his players had come into camp in good shape from a distance-running and lung-capacity standpoint. Landry would see how far we could run around the track in 12 minutes. To be considered in top shape, the linemen had to run at least 1.6 miles in 12 minutes and the defensive backs and wide receivers had to run at least 1.75 miles. It was a difficult pace to maintain for 12 minutes considering most players thought of themselves as sprinters, not distance men. If you had not been running your distance in the off-season and didn't run far enough on the test, you had to go for a penalty run with Coach Landry in the morning before practice.

Remember, we were training in Thousand Oaks, California—the desert where they filmed *Gunsmoke*. It was rugged, arid terrain. In the morning, we would see Coach Landry, a few guys who were six feet tall, 190 pounds, and a bunch of guys who were six feet six inches, 240 to 280 pounds, running off into the hills. The deal was this: If Coach Landry beat you, you had to add another day of penalty running.

It truly was a hilarious sight. Early in the morning, the group would take off before breakfast. After 30 minutes or so, off on the horizon, you would see what looked like a herd of elephants rambling towards the college over the hills and valleys. As the "herd" approached, you would see Coach Landry in the lead with a bunch of puffing big guys trailing right behind him. They were stirring up huge clouds of dust as they shuffled down the sandy desert trail. Knowing the consequence of being beaten was another day of early morning running with Coach Landry, all of a sudden, the last 100 yards, you would hear a lot of moaning and see this massive scramble of big ol' exhausted linemen doing their best to run past Coach Landry. I think sometimes I could see a small grin and a little chuckle on Coach Landry's face as he kept his hobbled but steady pace, watching the guys try to beat him across the finish line.

Every day there were always three or four guys who could never edge Coach out in that last futile sprint. I really think Coach Landry enjoyed his morning run and just wanted to have company. Whatever the motivation, the "Landry Mile" helped us win Super Bowls!

Slippery When Wet

Just a few years before I started playing pro football in 1970, the Astrodome was built in Houston. It was the first domed stadium in the U.S. and they installed a newly created artificial playing surface called Chemgrass. The surface was later renamed Astroturf because of its use in Houston.

The arrival of an artificial playing surface opened the door for different kinds of football shoes, not only for the games played indoors, but also for the games played outdoors on Astroturf.

The shoes that were best suited seemed to be rubber-cleated soccer shoes, which ultimately revolutionized the style of shoes used in games and started a running craze.

Unlike most players, I liked Astroturf. Even though at the end of the game the hide was torn off my knees and elbows, it was ideal for a player of my style. I liked all the traction you could get with the new soccer-type Astroturf shoes. Rubber cleats against the synthetic turf provided great traction. It was difficult to make really sharp cuts in soft grass using the old steel or nylon cleats in soft grass, because chunks would tear up. On Astroturf, I could make as sharp cuts and turns as my joints would allow.

Since one of my strengths was quickness, I used the incredible traction to my advantage to dodge the big guys and cut with, then smack the little guys—the ones more my size. It was a "fast track," and I liked it!

When open-air stadiums, like Candlestick Park, began installing Astroturf, a problem was created. No one had considered traction in the elements…rain or snow. On wet days, the Astroturf fields became skating rinks for the players—particularly defensive backs, who make their living backpedaling and reacting to guys running forward who knew where they where going. DBs had to cut and react fast, or we would end up on our tails more times than not.

We knew we had to make some adjustments, because in pro football there are no excuses for any mistakes. On Mondays in the film room, when the games were reviewed and analyzed by Coach Landry, saying "I slipped, Coach!" would get you laughed out of the room.

Charlie and I were determined to find a solution…at all costs. Astroturf was so new and it came on so fast that the shoe companies' technology departments (which were meager at best, at that time) were definitely behind the curve on finding a solution.

The whole league had been wearing the same old, traditional football shoes that had been around since the 1940s. Nothing had changed. Wilson and Riddell dominated. They had nylon-tipped steel cleats (a half-inch in diameter with a steel tip), designed only for grass fields. The cleats sometimes were one-half to one inch long, but the times were a-changin'!

We first tried to wear these same cleats on the wet Astroturf just as we did on grass to see if they would work…they didn't. We still slipped. We definitely didn't want to wear our Astroturf shoes, because we found they slipped, and we slid worse and the receivers could make catches. They were having field days! I needed to find a way to be able to cut and turn, or I would be gone.

We had a big playoff game coming up in San Fran. We prayed it would not rain…but it did. Our prayers were not answered. The field was wet, and it was that new damn Astroturf. We were in trouble. We did discover that when it rained hard there was better traction. Ironically, when the turf was completely saturated it was better than when it just rained a little. Of course, that day it rained just a little.

We thought, "Maybe it's not so bad; it's brand-new turf." When we went out for the pregame warmup we tested the field. It was slick as hell. We had to find a solution. We thought and thought…we had to win. We had to play well. We could not be embarrassed.

We decided we would go to extreme measures.

We knew this would work: We unscrewed the metal cleats down to just the post, which left a metal screw sticking out. Imagine having a screw coming out of the bottom of your shoe. Man, talk about traction. When we put our feet down, they were down. It was like wearing golf spikes on the football field.

The problem was the refs. We could not let them see the bottoms of our shoes. So if we made tackles, we had to jump up in a hurry. I tried not to step on any of my guys, because I knew it would do some damage. But I didn't worry too much about the Niners. We won and played well. Nobody on the Cowboys coaching staff knew we were doing it. No one told us to do it. Our commitment to winning and performing was an obsession that sometimes overruled good sense!

Ahead of His Time

The Landry System was created from Coach Landry's engineering mind. It was a very structured system with checks and balances. He used a philosophy of management by objectives, much like a business. Each Monday before analyzing our game films from Sunday, we would review our goals for the year. Coach Landry established our goals with the assistant coaches in the spring before the season started.

The goals, as he said, had to be realistic and obtainable. Then he defined the goals into categories of poor, average, and excellent. Coach Landry put the system in place, and we followed it to a tee.

Coach Landry's training methods were unorthodox by contemporary standards, but they proved successful. He wanted us stronger, so he hired strength-training coaches and we lifted. He wanted us to be faster than our opponents, so he hired track coaches and we sprinted.

Photos courtesy of www.CowboysWeekly.com

As conservative as Coach Landry appeared, he was really a very forward thinker. He was constantly looking in all corners for new ideas. His burning desire was to move the slick and shiny Dallas Cowboys, in their sliver and blue, ahead of the black and blue division's old-timer's pack back East where he started.

From a strategic standpoint he was far from conservative. He was very creative and innovative with new formations, putting people in motion and developing the first spread formations. He had his offensive linemen stand up while the offensive backs were moving around and changing positions before the lineup settled, statue-like, before the ball was snapped. This is where the Cowboys started to be described as a "finesse" team, which always irked me. He was definitely ahead of this time.

He also looked in areas where other teams did not look. He hired specialists from many fields you would not expect. He wanted us to have balance and flexibility, so he hired a martial arts expert to teach us Tai Chi. He wanted to make sure we were fast, so he hired a track coach from LSU, Boots Garland, to teach us to sprint.

But I think his most innovative area was the mental side of the game. He was always looking for a slight edge. Toward the end of my career, he installed a sensory deprivation tank in the training room. It was like a coffin filled with body-temperature salt water. It was a completely neutral environment—soundless, weightless. Your own highlight video played on a little screen right above your face. The theory was that while experiencing total relaxation, you would absorb what you were seeing with greater efficiency. It would reinforce your play.

I didn't use the tank very much. I didn't like it; I was claustrophobic. Our kickers seemed to use it the most. We found them floating around in Neverland more than any other players. But then again, kickers are usually a little different.

Out of the Blue
By Lee Roy Jordan

Coach Landry and I had a unique relationship. When Tom was hired as coach of the Cowboys, he had only been removed from playing for a few years. The latter part of his career he was a player-coach for the New York Giants. I came to the Cowboys during his fourth year as the head coach in Dallas.

Our relationship was more like player to player. I think Tom and I both felt the same way. A part of him still wanted to be out on the field. He continued to live his playing days through a few of his players, and I was one of them.

Tom knew that I was very committed to football and was a student of the game. I loved football. And during my college days at the University of Alabama with Bear Bryant, I considered coaching as a career. I had the same type thoughts with the Cowboys. In the off-season, I worked in the Cowboy offices breaking down and analyzing game films for Ernie Stautner, our defensive coordinator.

The Flex 4-3 Landry had designed matched my style perfectly. By design, the disciplined steps and hops of our defensive tackles and ends kept the opposing offensive linemen off me and allowed me to tango around the end and make tackles. The complexity and coordination of the Flex fit my size, strength, and speed at linebacker.

Improving performances was always on Tom's mind. He constantly made adjustments to help us win. But sometimes Tom's ideas or statements caught me off guard.

One of those times was on a gray morning in Philadelphia in late September 1971. I was sitting in quiet concentration in the front seat of the team bus. Across the aisle from me on the other front seat was Tom.

Meticulously preparing for every game, Coach Landry had a mind like a steel trap. *Photo courtesy of www.CowboysWeekly.com*

We were winding our way through the narrow streets on our way to play the Eagles. We generally did not talk very much on the way to games. And if we did, it was only about specific game strategy. We had an unspoken superstition about where we sat on the way to games. I always sat on the left and Tom on the right. Right now I was focused and ready to play.

As we neared the stadium, my concentration was broken when Tom leaned over and asked, "Lee Roy, why did you go to the right instead of the left on that quarterback sneak?"

I was puzzled by his question, but had an idea of where he was going.

"Do you mean our Green Bay game in '67?"

"Yes," he answered.

"Coach, that was four years ago."

Without expression, he merely answered, "I know."

He was talking about the Ice Bowl when we played for the 1967 NFC championship. It was a nationally televised game played on the frozen tundra in Green Bay. The outside game-time temperature read 13 degrees below zero. With the wind chill, it dipped as low as -46 during the game.

It also was a critical game in the history of the Cowboys. With a fourth-quarter loss to Green Bay, it continued our role as the team that could not win the big game.

We had the same fate the year before when we had lost to Green Bay 34-27 at the Cotton Bowl in Dallas. That loss also came in the fourth quarter with the Cowboys at the Green Bay 1-yard line. But the drive stalled, and we could never tie the score.

In the Ice Bowl the field was solid ice, and the situation was reversed. We were ahead 17-14 with Green Bay threatening at our 1-yard line with only seconds remaining.

Our goal-line defense dictated that I line up opposite from Bart Starr, Green Bay's Hall of Fame quarterback. I was favoring their strong-side gap and expecting a dive handoff to their fullback Chuck Mercein, who I thought would make a quick plunge into the line of scrimmage and then push toward the end zone.

Of course, that never happened.

When the ball was snapped, Starr hesitated and faked a bit to his left toward Mercein. That one move was just enough to lean me into the direction that I had expected the play to go. Then, at the last second, Starr dove back to his right and over the goal line for the winning touchdown.

His fake was in the direction of the run I anticipated, but instead they double-teamed Jethro Pugh and pushed him back. Starr alone went back to his right on the quarterback sneak. Four years later, Landry was pondering my move.

In my moment of hesitation and with Jethro skidding back, I had no chance to stop Starr. He was allowed the small space needed to sneak in and scored the winning touchdown and grabbed a berth for the Pack in the Super Bowl.

It was a game that would go down in history as one of the best ever. It was evident that it still stuck in Tom's craw.

"I don't know," was all I could say to him.

He was looking right at me and then just nodded his head and said, "Hmm."

We sat there in silence during the rest of the ride. Both of us stared straight ahead. We got off the bus, went to the field, played the Eagles, and won.

I am still not sure how Coach Landry used that bit of information I had given him on the bus ride, but I will never forget the question.

Face to Face With My Hero

During my second training camp with the Cowboys, I came face to face with one of my boyhood heroes from Arkansas—wide receiver Lance Alworth, who had been traded to Dallas before the season.

Before the start of his 10th year in professional football, the 30-year-old receiver, a seven-time All-Pro for the San Diego Chargers, had been traded to the Cowboys to replace Lance Rentzel. During the latter stages of his career, Alworth had lost some of the blazing speed, but he had retained his style and big-play ability. Even with his illustrious career, his ability to perform was being questioned. Some were unsure if he still "had it."

When I heard he had joined the team, I could not believe it. When he arrived, I wanted to go up and ask him for his autograph, but I thought it might be a little weird.

You see, growing up in Arkansas, which lacks big-time professional sports teams, the focus of sports fans always has been on the University of Arkansas. Razorbacks football players—including Lance—were legends to me as a youngster. And almost everybody in the state took great pride in the Hogs.

I dreamed of being a Razorback someday. Lance Alworth was my hero. As an agile and fast running back, he won games for Arkansas in a variety of ways. He was a 9.4 sprinter who dominated the old Southwest Conference, making amazing runs and easily speeding by frozen defenders on punts and kickoffs for touchdowns.

In junior high, I always wanted to wear his Razorbacks' No. 23, but I was never good enough. It was reserved for the stars of our teams.

So you can imagine how I felt the first day he dressed out for practice in Thousand Oaks. He was lined up in our man-to-man drill ready to run pass routes for the first time as a Dallas Cowboy

When Lance Alworth arrived at camp, I was thrilled; he was one of my boyhood heroes. *Photo by Russ Russell, courtesy of www.CowboysWeekly.com*

against our defensive backs. As we stood there waiting for the drill to start, I saw he was the fourth receiver in line. I gulped as I realized that I was the fourth guy in line to cover. I was going to go head to head with my hero! I almost passed out in a panic.

As the first guys in the drill took off, I tried to think of any way I could to get out of my place in line. But I was a second-year guy; I couldn't show any lack of confidence. I had to stay where I was.

As the guys in front of us took off, I thought about my grandparents and how they would have loved to see me going head to head with Lance Alworth—"Bambi" as he was known to the football world. I was nervous, and I did not know if I really wanted to cover him. If I tried to shut down my hero, that would help me make the team again, but if I covered him well, it might hurt his chances by showing how time had affected him. I certainly didn't want to be the one to bring him down. I was trapped.

As I prepared for the drill, I decided to treat him like any of my other challengers.

Quarterback Craig Morton had worked out a pass route with Lance for the drill. As we approached the line, I felt as though all of the activity on the practice field had come to a standstill, and all eyes—of the fans standing around the field, the coaches, and my fellow players—were on Lance and me.

When he got down into his stance—as I had seen him do a thousand times—he raised his head looked up right into my face. He smiled and then dropped his head, preparing to take off.

I did not know what to feel or think. My stomach flopped when Craig snapped the ball.

Lance was smooth off of the line and showcased the speed he was known for. He ran right at me.

Lance Alworth proved he still had "it" when he helped the Cowboys win Super Bowl VI in 1972. *Photo by Herb Roseworthy, courtesy of www.CowboysWeekly.com*

About 10 yards down the field he made a head fake and then took off on a deep streak route down the sideline. Not buying the fake, I sped up and closed the gap between us, and then ran with him stride for stride, because I knew I had to be right on Lance to have any chance to break up a pass from Craig, who was a deadly accurate passer.

Running alongside him, I remembered all of the acrobatic catches I had seen Lance grab effortlessly over the years that made stumbling defensive backs look silly. Now, I was potentially one of those victims.

So I did what I had been trained to do. I did not look back for the ball in the air, but I waited and watched his eyes. When I saw Lance look back, I turned to hone in on the ball.

I expected the ball to come between us, where Lance was looking and which was in a position where I felt I could knock it away or intercept it. But when I looked back, the ball was not on the inside trajectory. It was coming in over his other shoulder.

"Looking inside, it's impossible for him to catch that ball," I thought as the throw came down.

The ball was right on target, and somehow Lance, while he was looking inside, extended his arms and cradled the catch on the outside flawlessly.

Cheers erupted from everywhere around the field. I even thought I heard coach Tom Landry join in.

Lance had just made his first practice catch as a Cowboy. And he had made the impossible look easy as he had done often throughout his career. Only this time it was against me. That was the only time I wasn't upset after being beaten by a receiver.

Lance went on to become an integral part of our Super Bowl VI championship team that season. He even made the highlight film by grabbing a pass for the Cowboys' first touchdown in that game against the Dolphins. It was an incredible catch that showed his amazing agility.

After claiming his only Super Bowl ring, he played one more year and retired following the 1972 season.

Forearm Shiver

It seemed that I instinctively knew my opponent's most vulnerable spot on a hit. I focused my intensity and stored energy on that one specific spot. I never knew where I developed that skill. It may have been from my earlier years in football when I was much smaller than my opponents. To get a bigger player down, it took a focused shot with all my might at his weakest point. That was the only chance I had. As I grew and became stronger and faster, the force of my impact increased dramatically. In the early years, it always hurt me as much as them on a hit. Before long, things changed and my opponents saw stars more than I did, but my elbows and forearms were constantly scraped and battered.

One year the trainers suggested that I protect my bruised forearm with a piece of padding, overlaid with a piece of molded plastic. I thought I would give it a try.

In the off-season, the Cowboys trainers had acquired a new gadget and wanted to try it on me. It was a plastic molding oven. The toaster-sized device was filled with hot water and pieces of 1/8-inch-thick plastic were heated in the oven until the plastic became flexible. The plastic was then placed over the injured area and shaped to fit perfectly. When it cooled, it hardened.

The trainers fit the plastic piece over my bruised forearm with a piece of high-tech, impact-absorbing rubber underneath. The hard plastic distributed the impact all across the rubber, which lessened

My secret weapon—the forearm "pad"—is visible on my right arm. I used it liberally to put extra emphasis on my hits. *Photo courtesy of www.CowboysWeekly.com*

the pain and sped up the healing process. I used the forearm piece to aid in the recovery of my bruise, and then found it was an effective tool, even when my arm was well.

The combination of using both my forearm and my shoulder increased the force dramatically when I tackled someone. It worked particularly well when my forearm was not injured and I could use it as a weapon. This was just one more way to add an edge and inflict force, which is what the game was about for me.

After effectively jarring a few running backs and receivers, my new "protective" device became quite effective. One Sunday afternoon in Atlanta, however, I missed my target and hit the running back, not with my forearm, but with the point of my elbow. My elbow immediately swelled with a knot the size of a tennis ball. I had ruptured my elbow's bursa sack—a pouch of fluid that surrounds and lubricates the elbow. I found myself in the hospital in Dallas a week later, taking antibiotics intravenously to fight off an infection that had developed in my arm.

I was more careful after that, making sure I hurt them, not the other way around.

Yogi Cliff

Training camp was tough. I believed in going as hard as I could in practice. I tried to make practices close to game situations. When I practiced at a high level, it helped me perform at a high level in games. When I practiced hard, it forced others around me to do the same. If one of the receivers was not going full speed or was doggin' it in practice, I would give him a wake-up call—jolt him pretty good to let him know to pick up his tempo.

Two practices a day was an energy drain for some of the guys. Between the morning and afternoon practices, right after lunch, there was an hour or so break—long enough for me to take a recovery snooze. Mike Ditka, Dan Reeves, and Walt Garrison all roomed together, and instead of sleeping, they would play various games—darts, cards, and cribbage. They were the most competitive guys I've ever known. They competed with intensity just like they played and sometimes got mad at themselves or each other and would yell and scream, sometimes waking me from my rest time.

I tried several devices to help me recover between practices. I believed in maximizing every aspect of performance, which demanded that I also maximize rest and recovery when I could. At the end of the day my feet would ache. In the morning when I woke up, I am sure I looked like an old man the way I gingerly walked on my sore feet. To solve this problem I bought a vibrating, water-filled foot massager that I used at night before bed and again when I got up in the morning. I don't know how much it helped, but I felt it was an edge that others did not have.

Another area I tried to be more efficient in was sleep. I got a waterbed and had it moved into training camp to help me sleep and, hopefully, not feel as much pain when I rolled over on my beat-up body—another edge others did not have.

In the mid-1970s the Beatles were into transcendental meditation. They learned the practice through the Indian guru Maharishi Mahesh Yogi. It became a craze in America with folks learning how to meditate. I read about meditation and discovered that, while meditating, the mind drops into levels deeper than ordinary sleep and even produces brain waves that allow the body to experience a deeper and more restful sleep. The meditation took only 20 minutes twice a day.

"Ah ha!" I thought. "Man...concentrated rest. I am going to learn how to do this!"

In the off-season I looked around Dallas and found a two-week meditation course that taught the same technique the guru used with the Beatles. I thought I would give it a shot. I signed up for the course and went to my first lesson in a building off Turtle Creek in Dallas. There were about 10 or 12 other "meditators" in the class with me. Some of them looked pretty weird. Of course, I was the only pro football player and certainly did not let anyone in the group know I was a Dallas Cowboy.

The lesson was taught in a very dimly lit room with Indian music playing. The leader was a soft-spoken, very nice, older Indian man. He taught us about the foundation and religious aspects of meditation. I did not care about the religion; I was just looking for rest. I wanted him to get to the point. The classes during the week went fast.

The night before one of the last sessions, I had stayed out late and drank a few beers. When I meditated that next morning, I was a bit hung over. During the 20 minutes that I was sitting with my teacher right in front of me, I felt like the chair was turning on edge and my head was turning around like Regan in *The Exorcist*. It made me sick, and after the session I went outside and threw up. I learned not to drink then meditate.

By the end of the two weeks I had it down. I could close my eyes, repeat my "mantra"—a secret word they gave me based on my birthday and other personal facts—go into meditation mode, and wake up exactly 20 minutes later. Even today I can close my eyes, start my mantra and open my eyes again in 20 minutes, rested and ready to go. The course ended about a month before training camp.

I thought, "Another edge—more concentrated rest in less time. What a deal!"

When training camp began I woke up a little earlier than normal and meditated for 20 minutes before breakfast. After practice and lunch, during my normal "nap" time, I meditated and

The dorms at training camp were spartan, but comfortable.
Photo courtesy of www.CowboysWeekly.com

found I was more rested. In fact…I was too rested! I found myself
awake until 2 a.m. because I couldn't get to sleep. Everything takes
adjustment. I stopped my afternoon meditation sessions, and that
allowed me to go to sleep a little earlier at night.

I will never know exactly how much all these things affected my
game, but they sure didn't hurt.

Hot Bed

The dorms at training camp changed about the middle of my
career. California Lutheran College (CLC) built some new dorms

Folks in Thousand Oaks annually gathered to watch our blue and white scrimmage at training camp. *Photo courtesy of www.CowboysWeekly.com*

not too far from the original group. The new ones were nice, clean, and sterile. They didn't have the feel or memories, though, of the old, musty, original dorms that were attached to our meeting rooms.

Also in the middle of my career, I began to understand the value that promotion of the Cowboys brought to me personally. I drove a car for a dealership that cost me nothing. There were definitely perks that came along with being a member of a Super Bowl championship team.

One year I went out to California a week before camp started, to hang out with a long-time buddy of Charlie Waters' and mine, Mel Smith. Charlie and I met Mel in Dallas before he moved to California.

He was a very unique, cool, fun-time guy who lived in a little, cottage-type house near the beach in Santa Monica. He lived with a girl who was beautiful and young. She was the daughter of some famous Hollywood shrink in Beverly Hills who worked with movie stars.

Mel was a really different type of guy who pursued his own personal lifestyle, which moved him from place to place all over the U.S., doing acting or whatever he felt at the moment. At that time he wanted to be an actor and make movies.

Mel had a waterbed. The waterbed craze started in California and moved east. He had one of the first ones. During my stay with him, he let me sleep in it. He and his girl used another bedroom. It was really comfortable and I thought about how cool it would be to have one at training camp. When you are beat up from practice, wherever you lay, it hurts. A waterbed allows you to move around without putting too much pressure on any one spot. I thought, "I can sleep great and be really ready to go the next day."

After a few days of watching the girls on the beach, Mel drove me to camp. Driving toward CLC, where we lived during our month in camp, we first drove by a shopping center in Thousand Oaks, the town in which CLC is located. I saw, of all things, a waterbed store. Mel and I stopped and went in. I talked to the owner and convinced him to let me do a promotion for him one weekend, and for my time he would give me a waterbed for camp. He agreed. I thought, "Here we go!"

After a couple of weeks of camp, the delivery guys arrived with the bed. They set up a frame in my room and put the deflated bed in the frame and left. My Cowboys buddies watched the unloading with curiosity. It arrived on the Friday afternoon before our blue and white scrimmage, which was taking place the next day. All the folks from Thousand Oaks came out to watch the Cowboys perform. The coaches graded the film as if it were a real game. It was our first test and was full contact, at least as much as it could be against your own teammates. I did not try to knock anybody out!

I looked at that flat, plastic bed, deflated like a balloon, in its frame on the floor in my room. I needed to fill it up, so I borrowed a hose from our maintenance guy. I took the hose into our shared dorm bathroom and taped it to the tub faucet. I turned on the hot water and began to fill it up. We had a two-hour meeting that night. I thought by the time the meeting was over, the bed would be full of comforting, warm water.

Everybody found out I had a waterbed and came into my room before the meeting to check it out. They were all very jealous.

During the meeting I kept thinking, "This is going to be great! A waterbed is really going to help me relax and rest better, therefore, I will play better." The guys felt it would do the same. "What a good idea!" many told me.

After the meeting I rushed back to the room with several guys. The bed was full! I put a sheet on the bed and laid down on it. Thanks to the hot water, it was very warm. I thought, "Man, this feels great!" Some of the guys tried the bed and felt the warmth and told me how relaxing it felt. Boy, was this going to work wonders! It was worth going to all the trouble to get it, I thought.

Well, it was getting to be bedtime and I was ready to hop into my new, restful bed. "I'm going to have a great scrimmage tomorrow," I thought, "with all my rest." The warmth of the bed was very therapeutic. As a matter of fact…it started feeling really warm. I rolled over to another side to the bed. It was just as warm! It was starting to feel not only warm, but hot! I tossed and turned for about an hour. I was actually sweating! That bed was burning me up. I guess I should have mixed in some cold water and made the temperature of the bed cooler. Flopping around, I could not sleep at all! Some scrimmage I was going to have.

Finally I gave in. I moved all my sheets and blankets to the floor and slept in the little space beside the waterbed that occupied most of the room. I tossed and turned all night and did not sleep very much at all.

The next morning everybody asked how I slept. As I yawned, I told them "Great! The waterbed was incredible!"

I was lucky to have survived and did okay in the scrimmage considering how restful my sleep was. The best-laid plans…

Extra Padding

Most parts of our practice were competition-driven, which made it fun to me. Winning or losing individual battles in practice motivated me and kept things interesting, making life in pro football easier for me. As an established veteran performer, there was no constant scrutiny. The only pressure was game-time performance. I used practice to mentally and physically prepare for the next upcoming competition. When the offense was giving us a "look," I imagined myself in actual game conditions. In my mind I turned "our" receivers into "their" receivers to make the picture as real as possible. I therefore wanted our offense to give me a true impression of my upcoming opponents. If the receivers ran lazy, unrealistic, or "half-assed" routes, I gave them a jolt to let them know they needed to pick up the tempo. They understood and generally responded.

One of the fun parts of practice to me was the man-to-man coverage in what today is called the "red zone." It is usually considered to be from about the 20-yard line to the goal line. Because of the intensity and focus the drill demanded, it benefited guys on both sides of the ball. We always wanted to beat someone one on one.

With the end zone as a boundary, there is not a lot of area to cover. Game time matchups are considered primarily individual.

Tony Hill could really move. He "shake and baked" me right into the goal post.
Photo courtesy of www.CoboysWeekly.com

The action is quick and fast. Because the strike area is short, many times the safety cannot get over quickly enough to help. All the coverage, therefore, is forced to be more man to man.

Most often in practice, the safeties were generally not involved in much of the man-to-man coverage. In the red-zone drill, they were. It usually happened on a lighter Thursday practice. The safeties were brought into the heat of man-to-man coverage and I liked it.

All the defensive backs would line up face to face with the receiver and bump and run with him from close up. The receiver's first step was the most critical and where the battle was usually won or lost. The receiver "shakes and bakes" off the line of scrimmage, faking like he is going inside, then going outside or vice versa.

Tony Hill was one of the best ever in this territory as evidenced by his game-winning touchdown catch in our famous comeback against the Redskins in Texas Stadium in December of 1979. (That was the game in which Charlie Waters, who was injured and working as a broadcaster, exclaimed, "You gotta believe!") To win the game, Tony did a "shake and bake" that froze defensive back Lemar Parrish at the line of scrimmage, leaving Tony a step ahead in the end zone. He caught the pass on his fingertips, and we won the game with Rafael Septien's kick, 35-34.

In practice one cold December afternoon, it was my turn in the red zone. Remembering my old days at corner, I was concentrating, lined up, and readying myself to cover Tony. The ball was on about the 15-yard line. Roger Staubach was the QB. They had already discussed and decided on the route. Tony jogged over and lined up. I settled in right over him, almost helmet to helmet, and was focused right in the middle of his chest. DBs are taught early to concentrate on the middle of the chest and not to look at the head or in the eyes of a receiver. They can move their head and their eyes can fake you out, but the middle of their chest will always take you where they are going.

I was intense, but relaxed—ready to jam Tony as he came in off the ball. The key is not to get beaten on the first step to the inside, because that quick, short pass is an instant TD. The goal is to force the receiver to the outside, giving the DB control of the route. If he goes outside, the DB still needs to jam him long enough to throw the QB's timing off and set up a trap. If the receiver escapes outside fast, the DB is vulnerable to a fade route, which could succeed, but not as easily, because it takes a looping touch pass.

As you can see, the red zone drill was tense, but fun. My reaction had to be fast, and it was truly man vs. man. I liked the game.

I was prepared when Roger said, "Hut." Tony did a double move on me. The first move he started inside. I bit and instantly jammed him. He then made a quick move up and outside. I did not want him to get outside quickly either, so I jammed him to slow him down. I caught him on the shoulder pads. Tony had great coordination and quickness. The instant my hands touched his pads he shook and quickly broke back inside me. Damn!

I tried to jam him again, but missed. He was gone like a ghost, running free on a quick post route into the middle of the field. I ducked my head and exploded, trying my best to catch up with him. He had a step on me, so I accelerated and, after an instant, I felt I was closing. About that time, Rog rocketed his pass. I had very little chance of knocking it down, but I really pushed hard to close the gap between us.

The next thing I remembered was a noise going off in my head like a gong. Everything stopped instantly. I knew what had happened when everything went black. I had run into the goal post going full speed. Our practice goal post had pads that covered the front and back but left the middle exposed, exactly where I nailed it with the side of my head and shoulder. With the gong ringing in my head, I crumbled and fell to my knees, still holding on to the goal post as I slid to the ground.

The next thing I remember was the trainers pulling me up. Walking to the training room past my teammates, the guys held their giggles until they knew I was all right.

I was really mad—mad at myself and everyone else at the time—but I went into the training room to recover.

The next day, there were pads all the way around the goal posts. They told me that thing vibrated for 20 minutes. They called them "Cliff's Pads" and Cowboys owner Clint Murchison sent me a bill for putting a dent in his goal post. Very funny!

A Spot for Randy

The Cowboys' training facility off Forest Lane in Dallas was filled with the latest weight training and conditioning equipment available. Coach Landry hired an intense Jimmy Cagney lookalike named Alvin Roy to structure a new weight and conditioning program. His job was also to motivate and drive the players to top levels of conditioning. He did not have to push me. I wanted to get myself into the best possible condition so I could hit guys harder and not hurt myself. Charlie Waters and I pushed each other and competed to see who could lift the most. Alvin was one of those types of coaches I responded to. He would stand right in front of you, nose to nose, when you were on a weight machine and count the repetitions for you. Just when you thought you could do no more, he would say, "Just give me five more." He would count those extra five and then add a couple, even though you were nearing complete exhaustion. I owe a lot to Alvin for my early foundation on conditioning.

After Alvin, Coach Landry hired a physical scientist named Bob Ward to be the Cowboys conditioning coach. Bob took my athletic training to a different level both physically and mentally. He was quiet, but intense and very intelligent. He had a doctorate in physiology and was an expert in martial arts. He taught Charlie and me many things, including focus, balance, lifting, and thinking. He made us aware and taught us to concentrate on the most functionally important lift for our position in football—the power clean, which became Charlie's and my favorite and best lift.

On one hot, summer day close to training camp, Bob was gone and the weight area was empty. Since it was almost time for camp, most guys were taking a break before the intensity of two-a-days began. I was working a few reps of cleans just to stay tuned. The clean was predicated on explosion. The lift started with the weights on the ground. I held on to the bar, with my knees bent and head up, then powered everything I had into one motion upward. It was very similar to the thought process of hitting. I liked it and did it very well.

When I was just about finished, Randy White ambled in. It was one of his first years with the team. He was a hulk. I really liked Randy. He was an incredible player, who was extremely intense and very tough. He is one of those guys you always want on your side when things begin to get rough. He was the toughest football player I knew.

Randy, too, was a devout student of Bob Ward, and his favorite lift was the bench. I could picture Randy bench-pressing a Volkswagen if he wanted. That day he told me he wanted to max and asked if I could spot him. Normally, the heavy-lifting guys worked out with other similar-weight guys. I told him I would do my best. I asked him how much he was going for today. He told me 500 pounds. I gulped. That meant he would be laying flat on his back with me standing over him near his head and if he couldn't get the 500 pounds up, I would have to grab it and hold it off him, so he could get out. It would be awkward for me to hold that much weight. I was very nervous.

He said, "Don't worry. I can do it."

Randy White must have had much more confidence in my strength than I when he asked me to spot him on a bench press max. Lucky for him (and me) he never needed help with the lift. *Photo courtesy of www.CowboysWeekly.com*

All kinds of thoughts were going through my mind. What if I dropped it and smashed his chest? The press would be all over me for killing Randy White, our best pass rusher.

The lift began. He took a deep breath then hoisted the bar off the rack. The heavy weights bent the bar in an inverted "U." He immediately banged the bar down on his chest and, with a big grunt, pushed it back up.

Thank God!

I helped him steady it back onto the rack and breathed a sigh of relief. I never wanted to do that again. I did not like helping anyone bench press, let alone a hulk like Randy White.

Slow Motion

Charlie Waters and I were helping each other on our bench press in the weight room one day. We were working with heavy weights, but much less than Randy White would lift. It was another hot summer day in Dallas, and Charlie was going for his max with me spotting for him. I was standing at his head, slightly bent forward, as he lay on his back readying himself to lift. Like with Randy, I would grab the weight and put the bar back onto the rack if he couldn't make it. Charlie started his lift and pulled the bar off the rack. He let it down to his chest and then started back up. He was really struggling with the 300 pounds he was pushing up. He couldn't make it, so I grabbed for the bar to help him put it up on the rack.

My head was directly over his head. He was pushing very hard and grunting, with his mouth open. I was pulling the heavy weight up with all my might when I began to feel beads of sweat accumulating on my forehead.

The problem was that I could not let go of the bar to wipe the sweat off that was gathering on my forehead. I could feel the sweat drops growing and about to fall. I did not know what to do in that split second. Then it happened…

I could see the drop falling in slow motion, right towards the worst possible target—Charlie's mouth. With all that was going on, I didn't know what to do so I just yelled, "Watch out!"

Obviously, he didn't know what I was shouting about until the salty sweat drops fell right into his open mouth. He sputtered and spit and let go of the weight—dropping it onto his chest. Luckily I was

Charlie Waters lifts in the yard at CLC. Notice he didn't ask me to spot him. Cornerback Benny Barnes got that honor this day.

Photo courtesy of www.CowboysWeekly.com

holding it up enough that he could wriggle out. He was still spitting and gagging as he squirmed out. He ran to the Gatorade and washed his mouth out. I dropped the weights and they clattered to the floor. Not surprisingly, he didn't ask me to spot him again.

Negotiations With Tex

A few floors above the Playboy Club, at 6116 N. Central Expressway, was the Cowboys business office. Right across the expressway was the Southern Methodist University campus. It was a busy place during football season. Tucked away in the back part of the business office were the individual offices where the coaches studied films, put together computerized printouts that detailed our opponents' tendencies, and devised our game plan. They worked there in the off-season and whenever the players were not at the practice field. Our PR department was there as well, where Doug Todd and Kurt Mosier created our image and cranked out Cowboy propaganda. In the off-season, college players visited the offices before they signed their contracts with the team. This was also where players came, in agony, to renegotiate their contracts, mostly with Gil Brandt, but a very few with Tex Schramm. My first negotiations were with Gil, and it was always a test.

Times were different; few players had their own agents. Since there was no real "free agency," the players were tied to the team that had drafted or signed them. Your only option as a player was to ask to be traded. Your bargaining power was very limited. The Cowboys organization frowned on players who used agents and viewed them as disloyal. During my early years, I struggled to negotiate with Gil. When I began to have some clout, I asked to negotiate with Tex instead.

Negotiating with Tex was quite an experience. Tex ran the business side of the Cowboys for Clint Murchison, the owner. Tex made sure the Cowboys, even though they were located in the South,

Tex Schramm was a formidable opponent behind his big desk when it came time to renegotiate a contract. *Photo by Bucky Erwin, courtesy of www.CowboysWeekly.com*

The Dallas Cowboys headquarters were where Tex Schramm held court.
Photo courtesy of www.CowboysWeekly.com

ended up in the highest profile, most visible, lucrative division in all of the NFL—the elite Eastern Conference—along with New York, Philly, and Washington. Tex's strategic move caused animosity among blue-blood NFL purists. They demanded to know how an upstart silver and blue team from Texas could be in the same division as a team from New York. Tex Schramm—that's how. Tex was enshrined in the Pro Football Hall of Fame in 1991 thanks to his enormous influence on the Cowboys and professional football as a whole.

I only used an agent part of one year—my friend and prestigious Dallas attorney, David Witts. Tex didn't appreciate it. David was smart and did a good job, but we were getting nowhere with the leverage Tex enjoyed, so I finished the negotiation myself and did so every time afterward.

Without fail, when the time came to renegotiate, I was shown into Tex's office and as I sat and began my "inquisition," Tex pushed a button on his desk. I could see, out of the corner of my eye, the door to his office quietly close. Then, I swear, I could hear a vacuum-like sound sucking the air out. I felt like I was locked in a big freezer and there was no escape. Tex knew all the tricks.

Tex was a brilliant man and a skillful negotiator. If and when he finally gave in to my demands, I always felt like I left something on the table. I really think he only agreed because he liked me and not because of my negotiating skills. I did, one year, become the highest paid defensive back in the league.

Weak in the Knees

After all my years playing football, I am not hobbled and generally feel pretty good. But I was one of the lucky ones. Many former Cowboys have had all sorts of knee and hip replacements as well as a variety of other surgeries.

Charlie Waters was beaten up during his time on the gridiron. He has had a metal bracket inserted to keep the vertebrae in his back aligned properly. He also has had one of his knees replaced. During the off-season, Charlie was always in the hospital undergoing some kind of surgery most of the time on his ankles or elbows.

I was very fortunate in such a rough game that I only had one surgery on my knee—and that was because of a fluke on the practice field my freshman year. In spring practice I was holding a standing blocking dummy in the defensive backfield, enjoying a break from practice. I wasn't paying attention to the action on the field. One of the players, a big guy who was a senior but who had never played, came downfield during an offensive running drill and unnecessarily threw a high hip block on the dummy I was holding. As he rolled onto the dummy and then onto me, the impact bent my knee sideways. I heard a snap and found out afterward he had torn my medial cartilage. It was one of those rare times I relaxed on the field and paid the price. God blessed me throughout my career with durable genetics and the mentality of going full speed without fear at all times to help keep me off the table.

But visits to the training room after games became more frequent as my career progressed. I suffered a few cracked ribs and a broken thumb. There were a few times my face required stitches after it was busted open. Because of my style of hitting (leading with my head), I also suffered a couple of smashed vertebrae that ultimately led to my retirement.

But the injury that almost knocked me out of playing in the NFL came during my seventh season.

That year I did not go into training camp with my usual focus and intensity. I am not sure why, possibly because of off-the-field distractions. Yet after a few arduous weeks at Thousand Oaks, it was a great relief to actually play a game. Because I had established

My near-career-ending injury, which happened during a preseason game at Oakland, was caused by not playing at my normal pace—full speed. I never slacked off again in a game. *Photo courtesy of www.CowboysWeekly.com*

myself as a player, I did not look at preseason games like I did as a rookie where I had to prove myself in action. I only needed to improve my skills and hone my game.

Our first game was at Oakland. I did not like playing Oakland. Because their field was below sea level, you felt as though you were running on mush. It was a slow track, which took away my advantage of quickness and speed, and Raiders coach John Madden built his team around his home field conditions. The Raiders linemen were big guys, and it was hard to get out of their way to tackle the lumbering backs. It forced us into their game of just moving mass.

Madden's offensive strategy was not complex. He mainly ran simple plays with no finesse—just big backs with big linemen running right at you. Every now and then lefty Oakland quarterback Kenny Stabler attempted to keep us off balance by throwing a bomb or two toward the very speedy Cliff Branch or their excellent tight end Dave Casper.

To me it was a very slow and boring game. I was going in and out of the game, depending on how the rookie defensive backs were doing. In the fourth quarter of the game, on a third-and-long situation, Stabler ran an off-tackle running play to Marv Hubbard. When Marv hit the line, Randy White collared the oversized fullback and was trying to bull-dog him. Although I had been expecting a pass, I quickly read the play and headed toward the line of scrimmage and a collision.

In a regular-season game, I would have blasted Marv and prevented him from gaining another inch. But because it was an early preseason game, I decided to just run up to the stumbling mass of Randy and Marv and make sure Randy had things under control. But just as I was right next to the pile, Marv lunged forward a few inches. He caught me off guard and hit me right on my knee.

The impact was not fierce, just enough to knock me a bit off balance. In order not to fall, I turned and spun, but my cleats stuck in the tall, wet grass. As I was twirling, I had a strange feeling in my knee and fell to the ground. I got up and walked slowly back to where we were huddling and preparing for the next play.

Lee Roy Jordan called the defensive signals. But as I began to back into my position, my knee gave way and I fell to the ground.

"There must be a hole in the turf," I thought as I looked around me.

There was no hole, and I knew I was in trouble.

As the Raiders came to the line of scrimmage, I was lying on the field. I had never been in that position. I felt like a gladiator who had stumbled and was about to be pierced by his opponent's sword. A timeout was called, and the trainers came in and helped me off of the field.

I was on the bench surrounded by the medical staff and a doctor I did not know. It was the local orthopedic doctor we had pulled in because Marvin Knight was not around. He checked the stability of the knee—a procedure I had seen done many times. When he flexed my knee, it went into a position I knew it should not go. I became sick to my stomach.

As my stomach settled down, one thought entered my head, "Could my career be over? On such a fluke play?"

I was jolted out of my reflection by the doctor's voice.

"You tore your ligaments," the doctor pronounced.

I felt the anger rise up inside me. I was so mad at myself for slacking off on the play, and now my dream of professional football was over—by my own microsecond loss of focus and intensity.

The next morning I flew back to Dallas. On the plane ride back I was in another world. When I reached Dallas, I was driven to Muenster, Texas, about 90 miles north of Dallas, to see Marvin

Knight. Marvin was the longtime orthopedic surgeon for the Cowboys. He was the magician who kept the team glued together. He was an old-time blood-and-guts-tough, real Cowboys-type doctor. I felt he was the type of doctor who might just shoot me if I was hobbled, but I really trusted his expertise and opinion.

After X-rays and some twisting and turning of my knee, I held my breath for his diagnosis.

"You were lucky," he explained casually. "You stretched your medial collateral ligaments. You will be back."

I felt a wave of relief.

"Hell, your knee is not going to get you out off football, your neck is!" he exclaimed.

Prophetically, years later he would be proven true.

The recovery process was next. It would become one of the hardest things I have ever done. Marvin put a cast on my knee, and I lay in a hospital bed in Muenster going crazy for a week or so.

I couldn't wait to get back. When I returned to the practice field, my knee was still unstable. I went through a few weeks of arduous rehab and I missed the rest of the preseason. I was ready to test the knee in a regular-season game at Texas Stadium early in the 1976 season.

With my knee taped and still not 100 percent, I was tentative. But I made it through the game and knew I was on my way back. My knee improved daily, and so did my confidence. I played the rest of the season and made All-Pro.

But I learned a lesson. I made a promise to myself to always attack and never, ever let up on anything ever again.

Roughneck

The fines that are levied today from the rule change that punishes players for leading with their helmets would have broken me during my era. A good hit with my helmet on their chin always seemed to eliminate "hot-dogging" or "showboating" receivers. When a receiver knew there was a chance, when he leaped high into the air, that he could get knocked out by a ferocious hit when he came down, it took much of the cockiness away from otherwise confident receivers.

In today's game, sometimes receivers run routes with their chinstraps unbuttoned with no fear. The change in rules has opened up offenses and the scoring game. Over the years, the NFL competition committee has constantly attempted to handcuff defenses to allow more freedom for offenses and scoring. The public wants scoring or at least that is the perception of the NFL.

Football purists have always appreciated the intense physical nature and the overall toughness of the game. This sets football apart from all other sports. It is the foundation on which the game is built. Championships are built on great defenses. Great defenses are built on toughness and hard play with a subtle factor of intimidation built in. Showboating promotes individuals and takes away from the seriousness of the game. It is also contrary to the foundations of teamwork. Learning to work, and win, as a team is fundamental.

Coming with hard hits and leading with your helmet also comes with a price to the hitter as well as the "hitee." A bad neck took me out of football early, as predicted by our team doctor Marvin White. At the end of my career, I laid on the field a couple of times, unable to move. It brought a reality that led to my retirement.

On the Monday following Sunday games, the training room was usually full of beaten-up players. The two whirlpools would be filled with two or three guys with different parts of their bodies soaking. Some guys alternated their injured parts between a 50-

gallon tub of ice water to the hot water in the whirlpool—a training technique called "contrasting."

My time in the training room was generally due to my sore neck. I sat in "Cliff's neck machine" as the trainers called it. The chair had a frame built around it with a "noose" that hung down from the top of the frame. The noose fit completely around my head and latched under my chin, like I was hanging from the gallows. There was a motor under the seat that tightened the noose and pulled my head upward—stretching my neck—using my body weight as resistance. Theoretically, the machine helped stretch the vertebrae that had been smashed by leading with my head.

The machine pulled upward for about two minutes, then the tension released, and I had about 30 seconds to rest before it started up again. The entire treatment lasted about 15 minutes. Afterward, my neck generally felt better. And I felt taller...

Bud Grant Gets Tough

The first time I was picked to go to the Pro Bowl, I was very excited about my selection, but I wasn't sure how I would react to associating with the "enemy." Because of the violent nature of our business, I found it was easier to dislike my opponents when I met them on the field of battle. I wasn't sure how I would react to them when I would meet them in person the first time.

My first Pro Bowl was played in Miami. When all the players started arriving, they, surprisingly to me, acted as if they were all buddies who had not seen each other for a long time. Many of the guys had been to other Pro Bowls and other NFL functions where they had the chance to meet and get to know each other. Luckily for me, Lee Roy Jordan, who had been selected as well, knew many of the guys and introduced me. They all acted as if they had known me forever and treated me like "one of the boys." After that, the Pro Bowl became fun and something I would look forward to for the rest of my career.

My fifth Pro Bowl was played in Los Angeles. Minnesota's Bud Grant was the coach. The Vikings had lost the NFC Championship game to the Cowboys, which automatically made him the coach of the NFC Pro Bowl team.

I had heard of Coach Grant's loose style of coaching from my buddy, Hall of Famer Paul Krause. He told me that during hunting season, sometimes Grant would look up and see the geese or ducks flying over the practice field in Bloomington and he would say, "Guys, it's time to hit the blinds. Practice is over. Run some sprints." He would then leave and go duck hunting in the middle of the afternoon—quite a contrast to the very rigid timelines and strict practices of Tom Landry.

I had never been in that kind of fun, relaxed football environment. I had been trained that the only way to success was seriousness and busting tail. Bud proved there were different successful styles by making it to four Super Bowls. He never won the "Big One," though. Maybe that was the price of fun.

I did not know what to expect from him as the coach of the Pro Bowl. When we met as a group in the Rams' locker room, he told us we were going to have a good time and enjoy our accomplishment of making the Pro Bowl. We were going to have a relaxed, good time, but win the game. I did not understand how those two would work together.

We then broke up into our offensive and defensive groups. He came into the defense meeting, went to the chalkboard, and began to describe our defenses. I loved the strategy part of the game. I was very curious to see what other coaches in the NFL would run and how they approached the game. He told us that we were going to run two pass defenses: a simple man to man with me at free safety and a three-deep zone with me in the middle.

Bud Grant, head coach of the Minnesota Vikings, surprised me as coach of the NFC Pro Bowl team with his loose style. After playing for Coach Landry for so long, I had a hard time taking it easy during practice.
Photo courtesy of www.CowboysWeekly.com

Then he said, "Now let's go outside and practice."

My jaw dropped—no films, no computerized printouts or scouting reports. The defenses were what I had played in high school. I couldn't believe it. It was a complete contrast to the Landry "Flex," where every player was connected to and related to their teammates in a very coordinated fashion.

This was more like, "Line up and bring it, and we will handle anything you throw at us." I was uncomfortable with this style. This structure was more of an individual approach that relied on the individual skills more than the strength of the underlying framework of the defense. It was a type of defense that was more commonly used in the NFL than the more complex Flex.

I felt I was going to be under more pressure because I could not use my skills to try to confuse the QB, forcing him to try to guess which defense of our several I would be playing. In Bud's scheme, I was deep middle and that was it. It forced me to play pass defense more like the traditional style of Paul Krause, which was deep center field and not involved in the run game. I did not like it. It did not allow me to attack. It showed me how the Flex was perfectly suited for me.

We broke, went outside, and practice began. There was not much to learn, because all I had to do was line up deep, play the middle of the field, and stop the deep pass. It made me a bit nervous since I did not typically play this style.

We were also playing Terry Bradshaw, Lynn Swann, and many of the Steelers. I sure wanted another shot at them since they had just beat us in the Super Bowl a couple of weeks before. I would be facing Bradshaw again, this time just playing center field instead of trying to confuse him with our multi-defense scheme, which I don't think he went for anyway in the Super Bowl.

When our first practice had lasted about 45 minutes, Bud said practice was over and to line up for some wind sprints. I couldn't believe it was over so fast. I felt I needed more time. I found I had certainly developed a certain security in the long, rigid practice and the tons of information with which Landry's staff besieged us.

After the Pro Bowl team "sprinted" up and down the field a couple of times, some of the guys started to yell at Coach Grant, saying, "Bud, you are killing us. Don't make us run so much."

I laughed and could not believe what I was hearing. These guys were the All-Pros! Boy, was I trained differently.

Bud relented and said, "All right. Practice is over. Don't get into any trouble tonight. See you tomorrow."

I felt insecure and that I needed more work.

We did have fun in LA with Grant, played the game in the Coliseum, and won. I guess I learned a life lesson that you do not have to work yourself to death to win, but I never have been able to change my style.

Sorry, Officer!

Getting a good night's rest before the game was always very important to me. Some guys could stay up all night and then go out on the field the next day, suck it up, and perform. I could never do that. I felt that you only had a few times in your life to perform on the pro football field, and the drinking and partying could come later. If I didn't get my sleep, I did not perform well the next day.

Early in my career, the trainers had to give me sleeping pills the night before games because I was so excited and could not get the game off my mind.

During the latter part of my career, I lived on a cul-de-sac that backed up to a creek and a wooded park in the Bluffview area of Dallas. Peace and solitude were important to me. I loved to come home to a calm place from my hectic world.

I always thought it was important to go into a game focused and intense. Paradoxically, I felt it took being as relaxed and calm as possible before the game to perform well.

Quick decisions and action on a certain play were based on a foundation of information gathered from past experience and the previous week's massive data input from the coaches. Having a clear head meant faster and better choices. Success in football is still based on the quickest and most correct action taken.

To me, the best part of the week was the few hours before kickoff in the morning before a home game. I was at home in my seclusion in a peaceful environment with classical music playing in the background. The structure of classical music seemed to both relax me and help organize my state of being.

I sprinted down the tunnel. When I ran onto the field, the fans yelled, "Go, Cliff!" I was hit with the rush of adrenaline and excitement that running into Texas Stadium brings me, even to this day. It overcame all of my anxiety, and I knew I was ready to play.

I went out and caught a few punts and got back into my routine. The rest of the team came out later and everything was back to normal.

That day I had a good game, even though I had been robbed of my morning peace and had my routine disrupted. I did learn a lesson and was never late again.

Reverse Psychology

Though Coach Landry was not known for his spirited and motivational pregame speeches, he was effective. During the era I played, we won more games than any other team in the NFL. Results are what count. Without having all the right ingredients working at the same time, no team is successful. We had the talent and execution; Landry brought the motivation. He sometimes used unusual techniques to inspire us to win, but it worked for me. I was driven to excel by his psychology. Knowing how the Landry System worked, all the players felt insecure because we were just "cogs in the wheel." There was a poem on our training room wall that said there was no such thing as an "irreplaceable man"—everyone could be replaced. Landry had it there for a reason.

Moments before a game started, we were never driven by emotion, but always by logic. We had to stop certain receivers or running backs, or the offense had to execute on third down. Or sometimes he would tell us how important this game was and how we needed to win. The players who surrounded him understood and performed.

In the latter part of my career, near the end of the season, we were in the playoff hunt and were lined up to play the Redskins in RFK—my favorite game of the year. By beating the 'Skins, we could knock them out of the playoffs and we would be one more victory away from a playoff spot.

On Tuesday, when we began to prepare for the game after a day off, Coach Landry always talked about our upcoming game to set the emotional tone for our practice week ahead. He started by saying we could get to the playoffs this year, and it was one of our expected objectives defined at the beginning of the season. In the excellent category was going to the Super Bowl and winning. Then he said, "We have a tough schedule ahead with the Redskins, New York, and Philadelphia, and we need to win two out of the next three games to get to the playoffs."

I could not believe what I heard! I asked Charlie if he said what I thought he said. He told me, "Yes." I told Charlie, "He just gave us a way out." Coach did not have confidence that we could beat the 'Skins. I couldn't believe he would use that kind of motivation. I wanted him to say, "We need to go up to Washington and kick the Redskins' butts!" But he didn't. I don't think the other players were as affected as I was. This was an example of his brilliant, but obscure ways to motivate.

So what did we do? We flew up to Washington kicked the 'Skins' butts, won our last two games, and were in the playoffs. Go figure!

 **Emergency Quarterback**
By Charlie Waters

My eighth year in the league was a successful one, in that the Cowboys won the Super Bowl for the world championship. You've got to have great play from your quarterback to win the big prize. That year, we were very stable at that position. Hall of Famer Roger Staubach was in charge, Danny White was the heir apparent, and Jack Concannon was the seasoned third-string backup. If you asked the braintrust to name the fourth-string quarterback, it would have been me, since I played quarterback in college. I guess it was kind of flattering to think I was considered athletic enough to actually be on the depth chart as a quarterback, but I never anticipated playing QB in a pro game. That emergency never came to pass, but it came close.

One Sunday, Roger got knocked out, so the doctors decided to keep him out of practice that week and also the next game. Danny White would fill in nicely. The problem was, though, if Danny went down, Jack Concannon was not available, either. He had badly sprained his ankle in the previous week's preparation, and his status was doubtful to questionable.

So, on the unpublished depth chart, I was the backup quarterback for the upcoming game against the Chicago Bears. The week went as usual with Danny White running the entire practice every day, and by Saturday the backup quarterback (me) had not taken a snap. For that matter, no one had even talked to me about it. It seemed as though I was the only one who even knew or cared that I might be called into service at QB.

Concerned, I made it a point to sit at the front of the bus when we were shuttled to our Saturday practice site. Coach Landry was always the last one on and he always sat in the front seat by himself. When he arrived, I slid into the seat next to him.

"Charles," he greeted me. He always called me "Charles" when I startled him or when he was correcting me, which was most of the time.

"Coach, I've got a question."

"Okay. Shoot."

"If Danny gets hurt Sunday, what happens?" I asked.

"You are the quarterback," he confidently responded.

"Well…don't you think I oughta take a snap or two?"

Always prepared for every situation, Coach Landry looked me right in the eyes and said, "No."

The next five minutes was one of the best times I ever spent with Coach Landry. He proceeded to tell me a story, just like he was one of my beer-drinking buddies. He was far from a beer-drinking buddy. Actually, I don't ever remember having a "guy" conversation with Coach Landry. He just didn't do that. Maybe it was because of the military separation of officers and enlisted men that he had been used to.

He spoke of being caught in a similar situation while playing defensive back for the New York Giants. Tom Landry was also a quarterback in college who played defensive back in the pros. Seems like the Giants lost all three of their quarterbacks during one game and Tom Landry had to take the helm at the beginning of the fourth quarter having never taken a snap in practice. He made up plays in the huddle on offense and switched to defensive back while on defense. Incredibly, he was going both ways in the NFL! He was very descriptive and excited as he recounted the experience to me. He explained that the Giants came from two scores down to beat the Redskins and that he was responsible for both touchdowns—one running and the other passing.

After the game—jubilation! The next week all three quarterbacks were still hurt, so Coach Landry had to take all the snaps in practice. He even had a game plan with plays written on his wrist rather than drawing them up in the dirt. He prepared.

"Well," I asked. "How'd you do?"

"We got killed 50-0, so no snaps or preparation for you. I want you to go in cold!" he responded.

Danny made it through the game—thank goodness!

Buzzed in Green Bay

It was my ninth year; I had played in four Super Bowls. We had won two and lost two. When we ran the 20-yard sprints this year in training camp. I did not win them like I had in the years before. At first I thought that maybe I should work on my start then I realized the problem might be that I was slowing down.

A professional football player comes to grips with his mortality sooner than the normal human. Life is relative. You come into pro football right out of college at 21 and look at the "vets" who are in their late 20s as middle-aged men moving past their prime. You see the coaches as ancient when they are in their 40s and 50s. Speed and strength are the components by which you measure your life.

When you are fast and strong, you are young and virile, but when you begin to lose some speed and strength, you can see yourself growing old.

In my late 20s, I was reaching my peak in terms of experience and knowledge of the game. I had seen all the tricks. I knew how to handle the big, small, slow and fast. I was in excellent condition, but injuries were lingering a bit longer, which caused other associated injuries.

The game I played was full throttle, no holding back. That year I had been buzzed a couple of times on the field. When I tackled a big running back headfirst, sometimes it sent an electric wave through my system, and I had to lay on the ground a moment to recover. I knew this was not good. I had hurt the arch of my foot, which forced me to use my other leg more, which, in turn, caused me to pull my hamstring on that leg. Things were happening that had not happened before. I was forced to change my style and pick my shots instead of playing with freewheeling, reckless abandon. I did not like the new "Cliff Harris" style! I had to play smarter and more selective.

This was an important year. We had a very good team and a shot at another Super Bowl. Everything had to work right to get there, but I knew we had a chance to go to the "Big Show." We wanted a chance to redeem ourselves with those damn Steelers! We were on track, and each win brought us closer to another meeting with Pittsburgh, who beat us in Super Bowl X. We couldn't focus on Super Bowl XIII yet, because we had just lost two games to Minnesota and Miami. We needed to get back on track against Green Bay.

The week before the game we did our typical, total immersion— studying and knowing the Pack inside and out. It looked like easy pickins to me. We had to travel to the cold country, put it on 'em, then come home. They did not have a great team, but everyone got up for the 'Boys!

I really enjoyed playing the Pack, a team steeped in tradition. I knew Landry had coached with Lombardi. It was a cold but cloudy day, snowing a little. By the third quarter we had the game under control. A blitz was called, which meant I was covering the halfback if he went out on a pass. From all our study, I knew they would run a "circle in" route, where the halfback faked like he was going to the sidelines but then cut back and ran an inside route circling back into the middle of the field.

I knew what to expect when the ball was snapped. Coach Landry did not like it, but I always tried to lay off the receiver just a little to set the QB up, then pick the pass off when he was blitzed and had to throw in a hurry. Tom wanted me to cover the halfback so the QB would hold the ball, forcing a trap. I wanted the pick!

It was third-and-4. The ball was snapped and the play began. It unfolded just like I expected. The halfback faked outside and circled to the middle, but I was there waiting for him. The quarterback,

Bobby Douglass, was under pressure and rushed to unload the ball to the halfback. I thought I timed it perfectly, but I did not. When I went for the pick, the halfback turned his back to me, which forced me to hit him awkwardly. As we collided, I felt the lighting bolt through my system again. I succeeded in breaking up the pass, but the awkward hit jammed my head and neck.

I fell to the ground in pain, on my back, face up, but I could not move...anything, this time. I was scared. I remember snow falling on my face and, at the time, I thought, "I can't even brush the snow off my face. I am in trouble!"

It seemed like an eternity, and the snow kept falling on my face as people gathered around me. Then all of a sudden my feeling came back and I could move. I stood up and staggered off the field. My game and life had changed.

Feelin' No Pain

We had taken care of the Pack 42-14 and were riding the bus to our jet home. After my buzzing hit on the halfback, the pain was coming in waves through my body. It was a strange feeling. It started at my neck and then moved all of the way down my system to my feet. I cringed every time it happened. We got on the plane, and I was sitting on the aisle seat not talking much as all of the commotion associated with the victory was going on around me. The pain surprisingly continued and I was in my own world—I did not feel like celebrating. I spent the flight in my own world.

I was thinking about the future. I knew that in order to continue playing, I would have to carefully tackle and place my shots the way I did when I was in junior high and everyone was bigger than I was. That would definitely take some of the fun out of the game.

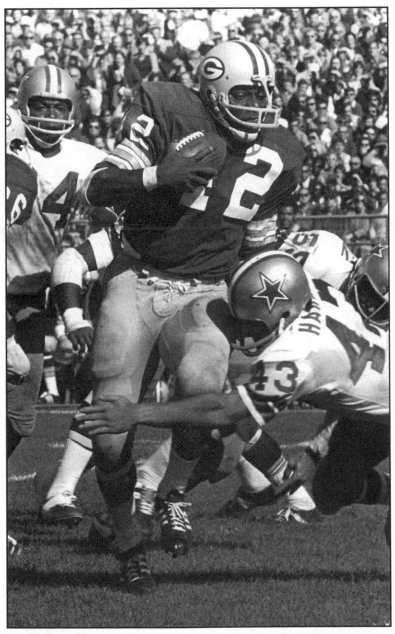

It was headfirst tackles like this one that caused my painful neck injury in Green Bay. *Photo courtesy of www.CowboysWeekly.com*

As the flight progressed, the pain increased and my back began to spasm. I needed some help, so Charlie Waters went up to the first-class section where the coaches, press, and doctors were sitting and told the doctors I was in pain. Drs. Marvin Knight and Pat Evans ambled back to check on me.

"Hurtin'?" Marvin asked when he came up to me.

"Yeah," I answered. "Some."

"Get up. We're going to take care of that pain. Let's walk to the back of the plane."

We fought our way through the celebration to the kitchen area in the back of the plane.

"Pull down your pants and bend over," he said.

"What?"

I was very puzzled. He told me he was going to give me two shots, one was Demerol for the pain and the other was a muscle relaxant to stop the spasms.

I did not argue; I was hurting so bad.

The flight attendants and my teammates watched and laughed as I bent over and showed my bare butt to everyone.

It didn't bother me; I was getting relief.

After he gave me the shot, I wandered back to my seat and slid into it. The pain was gone. I felt like I was on a different flight, this time "Over the Rainbow." I was feeling very good—no hurting, just happy. Even the painful reality of the end of my career temporarily vanished as well. I just sat in my seat, relaxed and smiling.

We arrived, and there was half a foot of snow on the ground. We had come home to a place that looked more like Green Bay than Dallas!

As I waited to get off of the plane, Marvin came back to check on me.

"How are you doing?"

"I'm fine," I told him. "I can drive myself home."

"No, you can't. I will find someone to take you."

Marvin came back and told me that Pat Donovan, one of our young offensive linemen, offered to take me home through the Dallas blizzard. As I got up to leave, Marvin put a full syringe in my pocket.

"You may need this for pain and may not be able to make it into the training room tomorrow with the snow," he explained, knowing that I knew how to give myself a shot because of my Army training as a medic and after years of watching my diabetic father take his insulin.

Donovan drove me home, dropped me off, and I went right to bed.

The next morning I woke up to a winter wonderland. I lived right off Bachman Creek in the Bluffview area of Dallas. The back of my living room was all glass and overlooked a park-like area of nothing but trees and a creek. On that day, the area was beautiful, all covered with snow. It was very quiet and peaceful. My neck was hurting some, and then I remembered the syringe Marvin had given me. The streets were covered with snow and there was no way I could get to the training room, which was on the other side of town. I decided to light a fire in my fireplace, put on some Rachmaninoff, and give myself the injection of painkiller. I did just that and sat enjoying the snow-covered landscape with a slight buzz all morning—not thinking about my future.

Quiet Confidence

It was a cool morning. A slight breeze was blowing into my face from the ocean. "It has been a long, exciting run," I thought. A glow from the morning sun was just brightening up the eastern sky at the edge of the Atlantic. In just a few hours, the whistle would blow in the Orange Bowl, and Super Bowl XIII would begin.

I was getting my mind right, sitting in the sand on the edge of the beach near our hotel in Miami. Leaning back against the wall that surrounded the hotel, I was lost in thought. It was my ninth year and fifth Super Bowl. Winning two and losing two, this game could be the defining moment of my career. I was thinking about my dad and wishing he could be there to see me play.

I looked out into the dim light and was surprised to see a dark figure moving along the water's edge. As the object came closer, I was happy to realize that it was just a man jogging in the early morning light. The runner had an uneven and hobbled pace, very similar to the familiar gait of Coach Landry. The jog slowed to a walk as the runner finished and headed in my direction toward the steps that led back to the hotel. It was, in fact, Coach Landry.

"Man," I thought, "I don't want to see him just now."

I thought about getting up and moving, but it was too late. There was never much idle chatter between Coach Landry and me. As he approached the steps, puffing a bit, he saw me sitting on the beach and looked surprised.

He said, "Up early, aren't you, Cliff?"

All I could think of to reply was, "Yes, sir."

He paused before he went up the steps, looked into my eyes, and said, "You need to have a big day today."

I told him I would be ready. Without emotion, he said, "I know," walked up the steps, and disappeared.

He always knew the fewest and best words to say that had the most impact. Saying "I know" was his way of saying that he had confidence in me. It was his unique way of inspiring me.

His intrusion into my solitude and mediation was certainly not what I had planned, but it took me in a different motivational

Thanks in part to Coach Landry's confidence in me, I always believed in myself. *Photo by Bucky Erwin, courtesy of www.CowboysWeekly.com*

direction than I had expected. I realized it was the same type of adjustment I had to make in my first game when it all began with Coach Landry nine years earlier.

His style was the way of the world. He would set things up for you, and then it was in your hands. I remembered my first preseason game when I was hoping for some inspiration and motivation from him in the form of a fired-up coach giving an impassioned speech. That never happened. It turned out that Coach Landry wasn't that kind of motivator. But I adjusted and grew to like it.

I got up and left the beach with confidence about the upcoming day.

That feeling carried over onto the field that day and I experienced complete silence and a peace just like the cool breeze on the edge of the ocean.

Mind Games

A sixth-round draft pick, Pat Toomay became a Cowboy at the same time I did. He was quite a character and a real intellectual. He told me a story once about his signing bonus Gil Brandt gave him. Pat asked for a Pontiac Grand Prix and Gil delivered, but the car had no radio and no air conditioning. Pat was too proud to complain, so he drove that car the entire hot Texas summer—with the windows down.

After his football career, Pat wrote several books and screenplays and even did a little acting. His first book, *The Crunch*, described three young guys' exploits during their rookie year. The three guys were Charlie, Pat, and me.

Pat viewed life and pro football from differently than I. For example, Pat was ahead of his time, one of the league's first mercenaries. He played for the money. I, on the other hand, was committed to the Cowboys.

The night before all of our home games, the team stayed at a Holiday Inn in Dallas. This was other example of Coach Landry's attempt to gain a mental edge over our opponents. He wanted us to focus on the game instead of the distractions at home. We also ate our pregame meal together at the hotel.

Pat was my roommate, and he always wanted to have discussions with me while we were supposed to be thinking only of the game. The topics never had anything to do with football. It was always something controversial like war, religion, or politics. I tried to ignore him and focus, but he could usually bait me into a debate. I don't think he cared which position he took, he just wanted to debate something.

One day Pat really tested me. I was resting on the bed getting my "mind right," while Pat flipped TV channels. (He liked to make

My longtime roommate Pat Toomay often tried to distract me from concentrating on the upcoming game—he rarely succeeded!

Photo courtesy of www.CowboysWeekly.com

fun of the preachers on TV, telling me they were all frauds. I couldn't argue with him on that one.) We were playing a big game against the 'Skins that afternoon and a playoff berth was in the balance.

My 'Skins nemesis was their Hall of Fame receiver, Charley Taylor. Man, he gave me nightmares. He was physically the toughest receiver I ever faced. He could take a hit and dish it out. He was their game-breaker, so I always wanted his number.

Deep in focus mode, I mistakenly said to Pat, "Man, when Charley Taylor comes across the middle today, I am going to lay him out!"

Pat said, "Hmmmm," and I knew he was going to lay something deep on me. He said, "Cliff, have you thought about what you are going to be doing when you quit football? Someday Charley Taylor won't be coming across the middle any more."

"What? Are you kidding me? That is not the way to think right now! Today, right now, I play football," I answered him. If I could have found something to throw at him, I would have, because he finally succeeded in breaking into my zone. Then we both laughed when I realized his bait had worked. I told him, "I'll be ready and Charley Taylor better be ready, too!" Pat may have succeeded in distracting me at the hotel, but when that first whistle blew, I was always focused.

CHAPTER FOUR

THE ENEMY

Blasted by a Kicker

One of the parts of the game I enjoyed most was returning kickoffs. Early in my career, I thought I was invincible and I relished the idea running them back blazing at full speed. In fact, I led the Cowboys and was always in the top of the NFL in kickoff return average and kickoff return yards. Today, my season average per return is still second only to Mel Renfro.

Most of the guys hated to be back there and were happy when I had the job. I knew that the more things I could do, the more valuable an asset I was to the team, so I could stick around. If possible, I was generally on the field most of the time.

For a time during my first year in the league, Duane Thomas and I were returning kicks. He was a phenomenal running back. At about six feet, two inches and 210 pounds, he had good speed and incredible moves that left defenders lying on their faces as he scooted

In the early part of my career, I liked nothing better than seeing open field in front of me when I was returning a kick. *Photo courtesy of www.CowboysWeekly.com*

past them. When we were back there together, he would make the call on who would go with the kickoff.

When he took the ball, he would bob and weave, and, at the same time, point at the guys he wanted me to block. We were an effective duo with our different styles. I would just take off straight up the field full speed. I always thought that the best way to run was to head north and south in a straight line, so I just picked a spot in the other end zone and took off for it.

In a 1971 preseason game against the New Orleans Saints, I was back there by myself and raring to go. We were playing at the

Cotton Bowl, where I loved to play. The fans were close to the field, and they were always vocal, which really fueled my fire.

The kicker for the Saints was still Tom Dempsey. In the previous season, he had kicked a 63-yard field goal against Detroit to beat the Lions 19-17. It was the longest field goal in NFL history at the time. Later, it was equaled. He was about six feet tall and 250 pounds, but what made him special was he had been born with half of a right foot and a deformed hand. He overcame his disability. In fact, it probably helped him in one respect.

He wore a special shoe with a squared-off end on his right foot. Many people believed it was illegally fitted with steel in the tip to give it added weight. He used it very effectively.

When Dempsey's kickoff came to me, I took off and I was thinking touchdown. I always believed I could score on every kickoff; I was not right often. On this kickoff, though, I was truly on my way. I hit the crease right up the middle and made the best of the blocking. I was flying. The field was wide open as I headed toward my spot in the end zone. The shortest line was to fly right by Dempsey, the only person who stood in my way.

With his disability and supposedly heavily weighted foot, I thought he obviously could not move very well.

"This will be a piece of cake," I thought as I turned on the jets.

Boy, was I wrong.

I put a casual juke on him. I did not think I needed much of a move. I wanted to make him think I was going by him on his left when I was going to go by him on the right and leave him grasping at air. All I needed was a momentary hesitation, and I would be by him. I put my move on him and expected him to bite.

But he didn't.

He exploded and firmly planted his helmet in the middle of my chest. I saw stars and felt all the air rush out. He really blasted me.

As I was lying on the ground trying to hide the pain, he looked down.

"Thought you were going by me, didn't you?" he chuckled.

I didn't say a word—just looked at him and shook my head. I had a newfound respect for the man with half a foot.

 ## Squashed
By Charlie Waters

Our competitive battles with the St. Louis Cardinals brought out the best and worst of both teams. The road to the NFC East Championship was through the Dallas Cowboys, and Don Coryell's 1970 Cardinals were well aware of it. Consequently, we always received a Herculean effort from them when we met. They had excellent personnel. At the skill positions, they had Jim Hart, Jim Otis, Terry Metcalf, Mel Gray, and Jackie Smith; and on the line they had Tom Banks, Conrad Dobler, and Dan Dierdorf. All of those guys hated us and made a point to make every game we played a physical war. It was bad enough trying to combat brute Jackie Smith, but Cliff's and my real fear was their All-Pro offensive linemen, especially Dobler and Dierdorf.

We never worried about linemen, except when we played the Cardinals. Both of those guys weighed 150 to 160 pounds more that we did, and they tried to kill us. On running plays when we weren't at the point of attack, as we pursued to help the cause, Dobler and Dierdorf would drop their blocking responsibilities and make a beeline to us, trying to blindside us and take our heads off. They must have graded out poorly during Dallas games because they would come off their block just to get a shot at us. It seemed like on every play, our heads were on a swivel—radar up—always on the lookout.

It's hard to get even with a man who weighs nearly twice what you weigh and can run just about as fast, but we tried.

Field goals and extra-point attempts were one time we could pay them back. Cliff rushed from the outside because of his quickness and burst of speed, but I occupied the 3 spot. My assignment was to wedge between the end and the tackle, trying to penetrate and draw the end's block. Dan Dierdorf was the end. On every kick, I'd line up over Dierdorf and I'd hit him as hard as I could, never attempting to block the kick, of course. That was one play on which he could not break his assignment for fear of a blocked kick. So, it was open season on Dierdorf.

I'd vary my shots. Sometimes I'd explode high, crushing his face mask with my helmet. Other times, I'd attack lower, around the midsection, trying to drive my shoulder through his stomach to his spine. It pleased me to hear him grunt after a stomach shot or to see blood trickle from his chin when I hit him high.

One game, played in St. Louis, the Cardinals had already attempted four kicks. Each time I had tried to pop Dan. I'm sure my shots were like fleas on an elephant—hardly noticeable.

On the fifth kick, when I lined up over Dierdorf, we made eye contact and he announced, "I'm gonna kill you!"

I laughed, trying to disguise my fear, as I took my sprinter's stance, ready to give my best shot and poised to take Dan's.

On the snap, I took one step forward and feigned like I was going to hit Dan high. He was ready and he lunged at me simultaneously. I dropped down to my knees and scrambled on all fours in an attempt to tunnel through Dan's massive legs. Initially, I caught him off guard and I actually thought for a nanosecond that I was going to get through cleanly and block the kick in the most unconventional way—crawling through Dan Dierdorf's legs.

Imagine this funny sight: Cardinals giant offensive lineman Dan Dierdorf (72) squashing Charlie Waters as he tries to scoot through Dierdorf's legs.
Photo courtesy of www.CowboysWeekly.com

Then I felt the force of all 325 pounds drop down on my back. My breath was expunged and my rib cage felt crushed. I pictured myself looking like Wyle E. Coyote after being flattened by a four-ton boulder. As Dan sat on me, I heard his unforgettable laugh, "You'll try anything."

Proving the President Wrong

In my second year with the Cowboys, we were on our way to the Super Bowl. Three years before, I had played in the Peanut Bowl, a NAIA bowl game between OBU and Livingstone State, held in Dothan, Alabama—the peanut capital of the world. Man, I was

excited; this was the big-time! We had a dominating defense—
arguably one of the best ever in the NFL—built on the framework
of All-Pros like Bob Lilly, Lee Roy Jordan, and Chuck Howley. They
had all been through the rough years with the Cowboys and were
hungry for a victory. I was the youngster in our elite secondary.
Statistically, we had the best secondary in the league that year. With
future Hall of Fame corners Mel Renfro and Herb Adderley
(formerly with Green Bay), we shut down every team's passing
offenses. Cornell Green had made All-Pro at both corner and safety.
Cornell was a very savvy and talented veteran. He was tutor and
mentor for both Charlie and me in our early years. We were ready
for the Dolphins.

Paul Warfield, a future Hall of Fame receiver for the Dolphins,
was their game-breaker. His forte was running inside pass routes. He
and I were headed for a collision course in this game. And no one
knew it except for the Dallas defensive braintrust and the guys who
were privy to our "Dallas Doomsday" game plan.

As usual, there was a lot of talk about the game in the press.
The week before the game, President Richard M. Nixon, who was a
big football fan, predicted the Dolphins were going to win because
Warfield was going to catch inside routes against the Cowboys. I
couldn't believe it when I read it in the papers. He was talking about
me getting beat. That was motivation!

After watching Warfield on film, I could understand why
Nixon made the prediction. He was truly an amazing athlete. He
consistently broke games open with acrobatic catches. I knew I
would have to play my best possible game to have a chance to match
his skills and prove the President wrong. I was ready and definitely
motivated to cover him.

I don't think Warfield expected too much trouble because I was
a new kid on the block. He was a seasoned and confident vet who

Bob Lilly (74) and the Doomsday Defense relentlessly heckled Dolphin quarterback Bob Griese. *Photo courtesy of www.Cowboys Weekly.com*

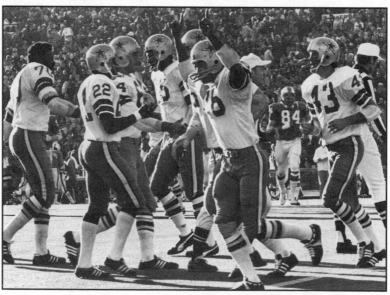

At the end of Super Bowl VI, I was glad to have proved President Nixon wrong. *Photo courtesy of www.Cowboys Weekly.com*

had never seen me play. He was also accustomed to playing against the old-style, deep-middle-zone free safeties of the time. I was about to introduce myself to him, "He'll know who I am after this game."

Similar to the way Larry Wilson of the Cardinals revolutionized the free safety position when he played, my style was different from that of other safeties. Normally, when receivers ran inside routes, most free safeties playing deep third would come up and tackle the wide-open receiver after he had already made the catch. The quick post inside route was a vulnerable spot for most defenses and would generally gain an easy 10 yards and sometimes even score. At the time, the safety mentality was to play centerfield, intercepting the deep pass and letting the guys up front make running play tackles. I did not like the centerfield approach. I wanted to be involved in every play—pass or run.

The two main pass defenses we ran in Super Bowl VI would ultimately be our best defenses for several years. One was a "34" and the other was a "48." On both I was responsible for the inside routes on the outside receiver, which was Paul Warfield, on both sides.

That meant if the inside route was going to be shut down, I would have to be the one to do it. In the very visible safety position, there is no middle ground; you are going to be the goat or the hero. I understood that fact.

When I heard President Nixon's comments, I said to myself, "I'm going to show you, Nixon, what will happen when they run inside routes."

Sure enough, we busted Warfield all day and beat the Dolphins decisively. We dominated on defense. Lilly, Jethro Pugh, and Larry Cole kept pressure on quarterback Bob Griese all day. When Griese looked for Warfield on the inside slant route, I made sure that door was shut. The instant he discovered that his favorite target was covered, he would pull the ball down, look up, and see Lilly or Cole bearing down on him. They were right in his face, either trapping him or forcing him to scramble all over the field. Warfield wound up catching just four passes and none for touchdowns. Our linebackers, Lee Roy, Chuck, and Dave Edwards, also held Larry Csonka and Jim Kiick, the Miami running game, in check.

Thanks to our defense, we crushed the Dolphins and won Super Bowl VI, 24-3. We were disappointed, though, when the Cowboys' highlight film came out that year and it featured mainly offense and showed very little of our defensive domination. But we knew how well we had played—so did Griese and Warfield. And I had the satisfaction of knowing I had proven our Commander-in-Chief wrong.

 The Truth
By Charlie Waters

One game against the Redskins, Charley Taylor was working his magic and toughness throughout the game. It was a major battle, like all of them were. Near the end, we led 7-3 as the 'Skins were driving down the field. Charley had already caught a few balls on me when the game boiled down to one last series—1st and goal on the 7.

We broke our huddle and I sauntered out to my lonely cornerback position, ill-equipped physically. The defense that was called left me isolated on Charley. "What? Who's calling the defenses? What happen to the old, reliable bracket double-team?" These were some of my thoughts as I lined up on Charley, face to face, one yard away. He smiled and winked at me. "Cute," I thought, as the ball was snapped on a quick count.

Charley faked inside, then spun back to the outside and forced his muscular body against mine, trying to gain a position of favor. I did not fall for his initial fake and I fought like the devil to hold my position. He pushed up the field to midway depth in the end zone, planted his left foot directly on top of mine and exploded toward the sideline. I was on him like a tick on a hound dog. We both drove to the sideline as I read his intentions perfectly.

Together, we whipped our heads around to search for the ball. It was coming just where I anticipated. I timed my leap perfectly and lunged into its flight path. Charley muscled his way to the same spot. We both fell in a heap onto the end zone paint. We tumbled and rolled together and ended up with Charley directly on top of me.

He had the ball. I had nothing. Nurturing a bruised ego, I thought, "I could not have covered him any better, but I still lost." Etched in my memory, I can, to this day, still see his seasoned mug behind that yellow facemask. He was smiling again, but a bit wider. He winked at me again, and then said, "Charlie, you will NEVER be able to cover me!"

He stayed on top of me, maybe anticipating a response, so I obliged him with, "Charley, I think you are right."

Enough said.

Payback

Football has been transformed over the decades. It has evolved from the pure extremely physical nature of the sport to a more performance-oriented form of entertainment. The early players cared less about publicity and more about contact. In the early years of NFL the game was rough and tough, and so were the players, like Hall of Famer Ernie Stautner who played without a facemask. Broken noses were commonplace in that era. To draw an illegal roughness penalty a player almost had to commit a felony.

To prove their toughness some of the hardcore old timers tested fate and their moxie by going out and getting hammered the night before games. The next day, even hungover, they showed up and played great. For example, Max McGee, one of Bart Starr's Green Bay receivers, partied the night before Super Bowl I and then had a big day, pulling in a couple of touchdowns. Billy Kilmer, the legendary night owl quarterback for the Washington Redskins, was the best example of staying out and most of the time still playing well the next day.

Even during my era, there were still guys in the league who could do that.

I couldn't.

I just wasn't made that way. I was consistent in the way I did things. I wanted to rest the night before and take advantage of every bit of stored energy. I never drank much beer during the week of practice and particularly the night before the game, because it was too hard on me and I did not want to have to suck it up for the game.

There was one time, however, when I broke my own rules before a big game. Coincidently it was before we played the Rams in October 1973 at the Coliseum, the stadium where the first Super Bowl had been played. I stayed out past curfew, and although I didn't drink that much, I partied with some friends from Thousand Oaks into the wee hours of the morning, then snuck back into my room, and crashed for a few hours of sleep. I paid for it the next day at Memorial Coliseum.

Quite frankly, it was one of the longest days we ever had in the defensive secondary when I was a Cowboy. We were beaten 37-31 when Rams quarterback John Hadl was finding open wide receiver Harold Jackson downfield time after time all day. Jackson had a field day and caught four touchdown passes.

Going into the game, Charlie Waters was playing out of position at left corner, the spot we expected Jackson to test. Charlie and I had watched Jackson on film from the previous week's game. We saw what appeared to be poor performances by unprepared defensive backs. Jackson streaked right by them as they watched the Hadl bombs fly over their outstretched arms and into the hands of a speeding Jackson for touchdown after touchdown. Charlie and I thought the defensive backs were just not reacting fast enough to Jackson's speed as he flew by them in the secondary.

"What in the world is going on here?" we thought as we watched Jackson make play after play.

We didn't realize how fast Jackson was and what kind of passes Hadl was throwing.

Hadl's pass was different than anything we had seen before. Instead of throwing a flatter trajectory on a post route, he threw an enormous, looping-arch pass 20 yards past Jackson, who could judge his speed as he was running alongside the defensive back. Then at the last second, Jackson sped up, separated himself from the defensive back, and caught the ball 10 yards past the nearest defender.

When the computer printouts were handed out at the beginning of the week for us to digest, the tendencies showed that the Rams ran 100 percent of the time on first down. Our game plan reflected that tendency, and Ernie Stautner and team devised a plan to stop the run, an attack that resembled an eight-man front that would completely eliminate run possibilities. That also meant very little or no pass rush on first down. It also meant just three defensive backs on pass coverage, and Charlie solely covering Harold. That was not a good combination to stop a world-class sprinter like Jackson and a bomber like Hadl.

For the first touchdown of the game, Jackson ran a quick stop-and-go, and then the race was on with Charlie trying to catch

Jackson before he reached the end zone. With no rush, Jackson blazed by Charlie straight up the field. I came from the middle of the field in pursuit.

Afterward Lee Roy Jordan—who was our defensive signal caller, cheerleader, and captain of the team—came back into the huddle at the beginning of the next series and said calmly, "OK, guys, let's go. Get Jackson and stop him."

After Jackson's next touchdown catch on another long bomb, Lee Roy said, "Guys, we've got to stop Jackson, now. Get it together back there."

Well, he got another one, and Lee Roy was beside himself because that just didn't happen to our defense. He looked right into my eyes and barked, "What the hell is going on back there?"

I didn't say anything. Charlie and I weren't sure what was happening.

That day was also 100 degrees in Los Angeles. And typically, when it is 100 degrees there, it doesn't feel like it. But for some reason—maybe because I had stayed out all night and the fact there was some smog—I was having a hard time breathing.

To add torture to the pain on one of the touchdown passes, I dove to grab Jackson and caught him from behind just as he went into the end zone. When we hit the ground, my chest landed on this cleated foot, which hit me hard in the ribs and cracked one of them. So, on the flight home after the game, not only was I humiliated, tired, and worn out as coach Tom Landry railed on us, but I also had a broken rib.

We got our chance for payback a little more than two months later in the first round of the playoff in Dallas. This time I got some sleep, and we were ready.

On the very first play of the game in Dallas, Los Angeles was on offense and was trying for a quick strike. Jackson was going to run one of his takeoff routes straight down the field into no man's land between Charlie and me. We had changed defenses, a short and long coverage where Charlie covered him short and I took him in his favorite area—deep, to better manage his speed.

As the first play developed, Jackson blazed up the field. Charlie jammed him a bit as he came off the line, covering the short area. As he entered my territory, I decided I wanted to send him a message. He attempted to streak past me. I swung my arm out hard as I could, caught his throat with it, and clotheslined him. His feet went straight up in the air. He lay there coughing, trying to catch his breath.

"It is going to be harder to get by today. I am going to do this to you all day," I explained as I stood over him.

Obviously, they threw a flag for a 15-yard penalty on me. I didn't care. It set the tone for the rest of the game.

We ended up beating them 27-16, and Hadl connected with Jackson only once and no touchdowns.

But even today, that payback game wasn't enough, because the Harold Jackson field day game still echoes in Charlie's and my mind.

Cheap Shot

There are certain unwritten rules in football that all players understand, although, to fans, the guys on the field are expected to be as tough as gladiators and battle with no mercy. However, there is a fine line between a good, solid hit when breaking up a pass and just taking a guy out. As a member of the defense you are always trying to force the offensive coordinator to deviate from his game plan by changing routes to avoid those kinds of hard collisions.

I was known as a tough but fair player, because I delivered hard but legitimate shots. From time to time, however, I delivered hits that sent a message to certain receivers or certain teams. These may have fallen into the borderline category. Occasionally, I felt they were necessary to assure a victory in that game or in future games, and I wanted to make sure that receivers kept that memory in the back of their minds.

One of these shots took place in Texas Stadium while we were playing quarterback Ron Jaworski and the Philadelphia Eagles.

Philadelphia had an exceptional tight end named Keith Krepfle. Like most guys in the position, he was the tough, dangerous bruiser on the offense, who was a blend of a linebacker, running back, and wide receiver. As more of a move-and-catch guy than a blocker, Krepfle could sneak around and grab a quick, unexpected pass. He was the type of tight end who could make a difference in the game.

I knew I had to factor him into my game plan and watch him while on the field.

So I decided I would mess with him a bit as I sometimes did with other players in his position. (Because tight ends usually were volatile personalities with attitudes, I would occasionally try to rile them up enough to where they would be so mad at me that they would drop the ball.)

Philadelphia's offense was on the field late in a game we had control of. We just had to maintain our momentum to win. The Eagles were looking to steal it back with what I read as a quick screen pass. I could also tell we had it under control with our upfront guys. All I needed to do was make sure that nothing unexpected, like the running back suddenly breaking free, happened.

Like a receiver is supposed to, Krepfle ran a streak route straight up the field in an attempt to take the defensive backs deep so the screen could develop at the line of scrimmage. This was also supposed to create space between the linebackers and the screen. I saw the screen developing, and I knew his was a fake route. As he came up beside me, something came over me. I don't know what made me do this, but I swung my elbow out and hit him right in the chin.

Hard!

His feet went straight out, and he landed on flat his back. It was a shot. You might call it a cheap shot, because he definitely wasn't expecting it. As he lay on the ground, he shook and cleared his head, I did not even look back, but kept running toward the line of scrimmage. I knew Krepfle was as mad as a hornet, and I knew he would be coming after me.

I waited a few seconds and then turned around to see this 230-pound guy coming at me full speed. Just as he was about to blast me, I grabbed him by the front of his jersey and used his momentum to send him to the ground in a move my dad taught me in judo. As he lay on his back on the ground for a second time, I put my forearm on his throat. I was just trying to hold him down and let him cool off. It wasn't working.

"You cheap-shot SOB," he gasped. "I am going to kick your ass."

I was perplexed because I knew there was some truth to what he was saying.

"Look, man, I am sorry," I said. "I didn't mean to do it."

About that time a flag came flying and almost hit us. I thought I was in real trouble. But in typical fashion, the avenger is caught, and the official penalized Krepfle for his retaliatory shot at me. They threw him out of the game and penalized the Eagles 15 yards for a personal foul. Yikes!

Dick Vermeil, the Eagles head coach, was going crazy on the sidelines. They ended up fining Vermeil as well.

"Didn't you see that cheap-shot hit that Cliff Harris made?" Vermeil shouted in disbelief at the referees.

Krepfle was fined $500, which was a lot at that time. But after the league reviewed the film, I ended up paying the fine instead of him. I did not mind.

So the next time we played, the Eagles were out to get me. And I knew it. They had a play designed for me! It was one of the first plays of the game.

Jaworski threw a long, deep pass, high in the air. It was almost like a punt. And he sent Harold Carmichael, the Eagles' tough six-foot-eight All-Pro wide receiver, deep down the middle. But he was not going for the reception; he was going to try to take me out while I was looking for the interception. Fortunately, I realized what he had planned and was ready when we collided.

Carmichael got me later in the game, though. During an off-tackle running play I was turned toward the action when he really dinged me on the back of the head with an elbow. So much for intimidating messages!

Zonk Felt No Pain

The program always had Larry Csonka listed at 6-foot-3, 237 pounds every time we played the Dolphins. I thought it was strange that his weight never varied from year to year. Always 237.

A few years after we had retired, I visited with Larry at a charity golf tournament we both were playing in. I told him that he sure seemed a lot bigger to me than the 237 the program had him listed. He laughed and told me he never weighed 237 even at his lightest, that he generally weighed around 270. Man, at least that explained why it hurt so much every time I hit with all I had at my bulky 194—and why he would drag me for four or five more yards when I had to get him down by myself.

Dolphins fullback Larry Csonka (39) was one tough customer. He never showed any reaction when my helmet smashed him in the nose.
Photo by Focus on Sport/Getty Images

He was a tough, quiet competitor who never showed very much emotion as he ran over you. I used to say tackling Larry Csonka was like trying to tackle a Volkswagen.

I will never forget a game we played in Miami. Larry carried the ball on an off-tackle play, and our defense had him surrounded. After he was gang-tackled, he dragged our big defensive linemen and a couple of linebackers slowly downfield. He was barely leaning forward when I came flying in from deep left field. There were guys hanging all over him. The only place on his body I could get to was his head, which was covered by a helmet.

I jumped in the air, lowered my head, and prepared to hit him with the top front of my helmet. To this day I still do not know why he did not duck his head as my helmet drew closer. The top of my helmet avoided the single bar on his headgear, which protected his mouth, and hit him square in the nose. The official blew the whistle, and the play was dead.

My face was close to his as the guys piled off of him. His nose began to drip blood. If you have ever been hit in the nose, the first thing you want to do after you are hit is rub it. Csonka was just staring ahead with a glazed look over his face as if he was in some kind of trance—but he never flinched or grimaced and never rubbed his nose—just stared straight ahead.

He got up, and I watched him as he made his way back to their huddle, because I knew at some point, he was going to have to rub his aching nose. He lined up in the huddle, and Bob Griese called the play. Blood trickled out of his nose over his lip, but he never touched it!

Wow. I had a new respect for Zonk!

Sunny-Day Jinx

Have you ever had a premonition of a bad day? Well, one bright and sunny Sunday, the Cardinals were coming to town, and I just had a feeling it was going to be a tough one.

Not only did we have to beat St. Louis to stay in the playoff hunt, we had to battle the red-hot high-octane Cardinals offense in the sun at our uniquely designed Texas Stadium with the famous hole in the roof.

Just thinking of the sun and the problems it had caused in past home games sent chills through my system. I remembered how I would line up to start a play in a movie theater-like darkness at one end of Texas Stadium and then as I backpedaled while following the action I would be hit with a brilliant blast of blindness at midfield. There were times when I lost everything—my line of sight, my feel of the play, and the ball—in the flashbulb effect of that sunlight, while the receiver, who ran a predetermined route, continued to execute the play unfazed.

Success at the position of safety dictates good vision and sharp analysis of the lightning-quick action once the play starts. Overcast days were the perfect playing conditions, but sunny days were not. With the bright sun, I thought it might be an omen of a testy day.

As if that weren't enough, it seemed that every time we played the St. Louis Cardinals and their quick-strike offense, it was always a bright and sunny day, which made me stay on edge the entire 60 minutes of the game no matter what the score was.

Jim Hart, the Cards' talented quarterback, led an arsenal of quick-scoring weapons—Terry Metcalf, an awesome running back who should be in the Hall of Fame; the speedy tight end J.V. Cain; and sprinter Mel Gray, a guy I didn't care for. My dislike for Gray may have been because he was so damn good, and that definitely motivated me to make sure I was on him the entire game.

The Cardinals offense usually couldn't overcome the team's weaker defense, and so they were always close but generally didn't win enough games to make the playoffs. As a member of the Cowboys defense, I never liked to leave anything up to Roger Staubach and our offense by expecting a high-scoring race. I wanted to win by stopping the opponent.

Needless to say, I knew on this particular late September Sunday it was going to be a fast-track day with plenty of footballs flying through the air. I had to be really on my game and not make

Lightning-fast Mel Gray managed to get under my skin every time we played the Cardinals. *Photo courtesy of www.CowboysWeekly.com*

any microsecond mental miscues with my decisions, because Gray would be by me in a flash. I needed all of the advantages I could get in the passing war I was expecting. My skills would be tested to the max—and I wasn't planning on making any mistakes.

As a free safety, I had to play with ferocity and intensity, but I still had to play intelligently and not make errors by overcommitting. Mistakes and misjudgments meant more than just missed tackles or pass receptions for me. Being beaten generally meant touchdowns, momentum changes, and the possible loss of the game!

All of these things weighed on my mind as I got ready for the game. I couldn't get the suspicion of bad things to come out of my head. It was so overpowering that I decided I needed to knock Gray out of the game. That was the only solution I could devise for my sunshine problem.

I was already jittery before the game but calmed down and settled in after play began. Then came my first "mistake."

We had stopped the Cardinals and forced them to punt. I was on the punt return team and I lined up on the outside for the punt block that Mike Ditka, then the special teams coach, had designed. When the ball was snapped, I broke inside Benny Barnes, one of the best cornerbacks the Cowboys ever had, just as planned, and my man went outside. I was running full speed toward the punter.

Just as the punter dropped the ball, I dove to block it. I had it! Then I felt a crushing blow from behind me. I was knocked off balance by the deep protector and smashed into the punter. Flags flew. I was penalized for roughing the punter. I couldn't believe it. The Cards got the ball back. I was really upset and mad at myself and the officials as I lined up to face the Cardinals offense again.

I felt the Cards had been given a fresh breath of air through the penalty, and I wanted to get the momentum back. On second down,

Hart snapped the ball and the movement on the line was somewhat confusing to me. From the beginning of the play, I knew something was different about it. I watched carefully, trying to figure out what they planned to do—and I watched Gray move. Then it clicked! A reverse to Mel Gray!

Gray received the ball about midfield and was running parallel to the line of scrimmage and headed toward our sideline. I saw the play developing and took off at the best angle that would lead to a collision with Gray. Here was my shot! Dan Dierdorf, the Cardinals' Hall of Fame tackle, was leading the play and about to head up our sidelines. Gray faked inside on Dierdorf as though he was going to cut back. I knew, though, he was going outside and anticipated his ploy. I was going to nail him as soon as he came outside of his big lead blocker and turned upfield. I timed it just right. He had played right into my hands!

The moment he stuck his head outside of Dierdorf's shadow, I was there. I had him. I was going to nail him. For some unknown reason, I swung my fist right at Gray's face, targeting his nose.

"This is going to be pretty painful for him," I thought.

But I was wrong.

At the last split-second he ducked his head. Oh, oh! My fist, with my thumb leading, hit Gray's helmet. The impact immediately broke and compressed the bone of my thumb back into itself. A lightning bolt shot up my arm. And I almost blacked out. Gray lay stunned on the ground.

About that time a flag came floating down to add to my humiliation. I was not only penalized and kicked out of the game for my second personal foul, but had broken my damn thumb!

The bad feeling had come true. It was the sunny-day jinx—for me. The Cowboys still managed to win 19-14.

Silent Thoughts Amid a Mad Frenzy

Focus and concentration are the most critical components to playing at the high levels professional sports demand. Ever since my days at Ouachita—when, even though the stands were full, there were not very many fans—no matter how noisy the stadium was, when I was on the field I played in a world of complete silence. I heard no crowd noise, screaming fans, or any cheering.

That silent place is important in any sport or anywhere that demands a consuming focus. It also becomes addictive. Going to that world of focus and pressure on Sundays was something that dominated my existence. Putting myself into the most stressful positions possible became not only exciting, but also addictive.

To some players, myself included, existing in that quiet, but frantic and stress-filled world of focus is peaceful. It was a place I could go and escape reality. For some players it became a problem when the game ended, and they chose to go back through the use of drugs. On our off days, Charlie Waters and I chose full speed on dirt bikes as our escape.

Today's players still feel the peace that exists when they are addicted to high-pressure situations, and that is why they sometimes get into trouble with their attempts to escape the "real" world that exists outside the bounds of the football stadium.

When I was playing a game, I often wouldn't hear the fans in Texas Stadium. People may not realize this: I could only hear my named announced by the PA announcer after a play ended as I was walking back to the huddle. During the play, I was so focused all I heard was silence!

I actually caught myself in that silent world on a critical play one Sunday afternoon. We were playing the St. Louis Cardinals in Texas Stadium. The situation was critical in the fourth quarter, and

When the whistle blew and the game started I was all focused intensity. I blocked out all noise and distractions and concentrated on my job—inflicting pain on my enemies. *Photo courtesy of www.CowboysWeekly.com*

the Cards had third and long. The defensive call that came in from the sidelines was a Flex Weak 35. I gulped. That meant we were eliminating the outside receivers by double covering with either our linebackers or our strong safety. With the focus on the outside guys, that meant my free safety position was the only one that was isolated in man-on-man coverage on the tight end with no help. It was a deceptive defensive call that was designed to look like another coverage and confuse the quarterback long enough for Randy White or Harvey Martin to zero in on him. Jim Hart was the Cardinals' savvy veteran QB. J.V. Cain was their big, speedy tight end. When the play started, I faked to the weak side but had to jump on Cain fast as he was taking off full speed up field. I was trying to disguise the coverage because I didn't want Hart to recognize my isolation and realize what was transpiring until it was too late for him.

Cain made a move to the post route then cut back to the corner. I was the only person anywhere close to Cain. He was running full speed right up the middle of the field, while the other receivers ran streak routes down the sidelines. It was obvious to everyone—Hart and everyone in the stadium—that I was in fact man to man on J.V. It was important that I stayed with him in this very difficult defense, because I had no help anywhere from anybody. I was astounded at what happened next.

When I was backpedaling, mirroring his actions, he sped up. To keep up, I turned and broke out of my backpedal. As we were both running down the field at full speed, suddenly everything seemed to slow down. I felt like we were moving in slow motion and I caught myself thinking about how quiet it was in my mind. I was thinking, "I am covering this guy perfectly. My form is just right. I've got him!"

Then I thought to myself, "My gosh, I can't believe I am thinking this."

About that time, Hart released the pass headed toward Cain. Right at the last moment, I leaped into the air and batted the ball away. I was lucky to have made the play because, in reality, I had broken my own concentration by thinking how well I was concentrating.

by the ski purists for its cold temperatures and deep powder. It was not a very developed resort but had great potential because it had more snowfall than any other place in Colorado.

Ditka and the boys decided they needed some promotion so they chartered an old C-47, a propeller plane used in World War II to drop paratroopers, and invited some of us to go skiing after football season ended.

Although none of us had ever really skied before, about 10 or 12 of us decided on a whim to take them up on their offer. The group consisted of Dan Reeves, Walt Garrison, Lee Roy Jordan, Charlie Waters, a few others, and me. Most brought their wives.

The plane left from a hangar at Love Field. As we were walking on the runway and up the stairs to board, we all looked at the very plane skeptically. It did look like it was old enough to actually have been used in World War II. There was some trepidation, but thanks to peer pressure, everyone got on board and said their prayers.

We imagined the pilots in their leather caps looked like Snoopy or the Red Baron. They fired up the old engines, and the plane shook and rattled, and oil ran down the wings as black smoke pillowed out of the sputtering engines. We taxied down the runway.

"This is where I am going to die," I thought as the plane took off. "Coach Landry is about to lose the core of his team."

When we got airborne, the plane was still rattling and very drafty. Some guys got airsick. But soon the liquor flowed, and the ride got easier.

When we landed, some guys got out and kissed the ground. We then loaded up on an old bus and drove to the resort on winding roads through Wolf Creek Pass where there was more snow than I had ever seen.

Wolf Creek had the most snow, but it also was the coldest spot in Colorado as well. I think the temperature was 10 degrees below zero when we went out the next day. We all gathered at the small ski lodge

At Mike Ditka's Colorado resort, I learned to ski the hard way.
Photo courtesy of Cliff Harris

at the base of the mountain and began stumbling around awkwardly trying on heavy ski boots and getting fitted with seven-foot skis.

In typical Ditka style, he had bought all the perfect ski equipment for the trip. He was all decked out in the latest skis, the best poles, and the warmest clothes. His suit was light blue and perfectly matched his brand-new skis. I thought he must be very good. There was an option to go partway up the mountain or to the top. Ditka went right to the top of the mountain, ready to take it on.

"Hey, there's powder up there at the top, so it will be harder for beginners," the other skiers warned him.

Ditka took off anyway. He didn't make it very far before he fell and struggled to get up. On the steep slope he fell and fell again. Along with the high altitude, he was really struggling and was becoming angry in typical Ditka fashion. After 10 or so falls, he took his ski poles and snapped them in two over his knee. He then struggled the rest of the way down with no poles. When he got to the bottom of the hill, he was covered in snow and soaking wet from perspiration. As he stomped past us, no one said anything—we all knew better. Nobody messed with big Mike when he was mad!

I tried a different attack. I had some confidence because of growing up in Hot Springs. I had learned to water ski at an early age and was pretty good. I mistakenly thought that meant that I could ski in snow. I clumsily took the lift three-quarters of the way up the mountain. I slipped and slid off of the lift, but then immediately started heading straight down the slope.

"This isn't too hard," I thought, as I tucked down like I had seen skiers do on TV.

I kept picking up speed and then more speed. The hill had a series of steep slopes followed by a flat area, and then another steeper slope and a longer flatter area. Each time I went down a level, I sped up—and I didn't know how to slow down. As I streaked past other skiers, they yelled at me.

"Slow down!"

"Just fall down to stop!"

"I wish I knew how," I thought as I blazed down the mountainside.

Finally in the middle of one of the slopes, I fell and tumbled down the mountain. My skis and poles went flying as I slid about 200 yards. When I came to a stop, I was covered from head to toe in snow. As I got up, I spit out some of the snow that had made it into my mouth.

It felt like I had rolled for a half-mile, but luckily I landed unscathed in the middle of one of the flatter stretches. People who had seen the fall rushed over to me because they were worried I was hurt. Thanks to my conditioning I was fine, but I could have been killed.

Even with the fall, that trek hooked me on skiing. I went back to Wolf Creek the next year with Pat Toomay, who was a very good skier, took lessons, and slowed down.

Walt Garrison was a cowboy in two ways—on the football field and in the rodeo arena. In fact, his Cowboys signing bonus in 1966 included a horse trailer. *Photo by Russ Russell, courtesy of www.CowboysWeekly.com*

Rodeo Moonlighting
By Walt Garrison

Both football and rodeo kept me in shape. After football I would go to Fort Worth and San Antonio for rodeo and it would take me two weeks to get into bulldogging, or steer wrestling, shape where my arm wasn't sore. I used different muscles in the two sports. In bulldogging, I had to be more agile. I needed some coordination, but not a lot.

When I was a rookie for the Cowboys, I used to rodeo on Saturday nights at Mansfield's Cowbell Arena—where they had a weekly rodeo—before home games. As a team, the Cowboys met Saturday afternoon and then ate together at 6 p.m. at the Holiday Inn over on Central. I ate dinner and was gone. I had to be back to the hotel by the 11 p.m. curfew.

Bill, a buddy of mine, took my horse to the rodeo for me. I'd go bulldog and then come back. I did that two or three times without the Cowboys knowing, until someone called the Cowboys and said, "It is so nice that you let Walt come out and bulldog the night before the game."

After that call, Coach Landry called me into his office.

"We don't do that," he said.

"Okay," I replied.

And that was the end of my in-season bulldogging.

Wildfire

Dwight Douglas "D.D." Lewis was a star at Mississippi State and remains a legend at the Southeastern Conference school. His friendly, country-boy nature belied his intense competitiveness. Although he was not very big or fast, D.D. was an excellent athlete and a savvy player who grasped the Landry System. He was drafted in 1968 and played weak-side linebacker for the Cowboys after All-Pro Chuck Howley called it quits following the 1973 season.

"Loomis," as he was nicknamed by teammate Dave Edwards, was always ready for a good time. In the 1970s, when we played for the Cowboys, he and I would annually celebrate our birthdays (which fell in the same month) with a few shots of tequila in some dark, little bar after practice. I would feel terrible the next day. D.D. later had some drinking problems. But today, after whipping them, he is a card-carrying member of Alcoholics Anonymous in good standing.

D.D. was like the majority of Cowboys players during that era. We were all paid well, but none made enough to live extravagant lifestyles. D.D. did step up a bit and bought a lake house on Lake Lavon, which was located on the outskirts of northeast Dallas. His main complaint about his "extravagance" was the limited amount of time he had to spend up there.

Going to training camp in July in Thousand Oaks and often playing or practicing football through the Super Bowl in late January did not allow much free time for the players or coaches. D.D. had mentioned that he wanted me to see his lake house and how cool it was. During the week, our team meetings started at 9 a.m. and practice ended with showers at 6:30 p.m. We flew off to games on the weekends or had to stay at a hotel on Saturday night before home games. So hanging out at the lake house was nearly impossible during the football or practice seasons.

One morning during a football meeting, D.D. asked me to drive up with him and see his place on the lake during our lunch break. He said if we took off right after our morning meeting, which ended at around noon, that we could zoom up there, check it out and make it back before Mike Ditka called roll at the start of our next session. Our afternoon session with Coach Landry began promptly at 1 p.m, with both the offense and defense together. Of course, there were fines imposed on those who arrived after Ditka called the first name. Feeling adventuresome, I agreed to give it a shot and took off with D.D. on the trip to his lake house.

The tricky part was to drive up, see the house, and still have enough time to wolf down a bit of lunch, get our ankles taped by trainers, and put our football pants on before sitting down to the afternoon session. Mere logistics, we thought! At the end of the morning meeting, we screamed off blazing in D.D.'s BMW toward the lake. It was a lark. That was D.D.'s style at the time.

It took us about 20 minutes to get up there. We had an hour to do everything, so we figured we did not have a whole lot of time to mess around. D.D.'s house really was pretty cool. It was a small, but quaint, cottage on five acres of land on one of the lake's points. D.D. wanted to drive around the point, and then we would take off back to camp.

Since it was the fall, all the grass surrounding the house was tall, brown, and dead. We drove on what looked like a little path around the backside of his house. As we were driving, I glanced back and noticed some smoke coming up from the grass in the trail behind us. I told D.D. We looked back and a small fire was starting. After D.D stopped the car, we jumped out and ran back to the spot and began to try to put it out by stomping on it with our feet. I looked further back up the trail and noticed another fire had started. We were in trouble. Then, when I looked around, there was a fire under D.D.'s car! I ran and jumped in and started backing it up fast to a place where the grass was not so high.

Apparently the catalytic converter on the bottom of his car was very hot and had ignited the grass. By this time, D.D. was frantically beating the fire with his jacket. I jumped in, backed up, and parked his car 50 yards away, grabbed one of the floor mats and ran back to help. I decided to take a short cut and attempted to hurdle a barbed-wire fence in front of me, but I had on blue jeans that did not allow for much flexibility. As I leaped over the fence, one of the barbs caught my pants leg and I tumbled and hit the ground hard. I was thinking, "Man, what have we gotten into?"

Here I was lying on the ground, covered with soot, and smelling like smoke. I had a gash in my leg. The fire was out of control. And practice was about to start 20 miles away—what a mess! The fire spread. There was no one around to help. We were in big trouble! We decided to leave and go for help. We drove up the road to a neighbor's house and ask them to call the neighborhood fire department. We were losing precious time.

We went back and tried to beat out the fire, which was now blazing. Just then an old-time fire truck pulled into D.D.'s yard. It was the Lavon Volunteer Fire Department. So we took off back to practice. No laughing now, just flying low.

We sped back in record time and both ran into the field house. It was quiet. The meeting was in progress with the doors closed. D.D. went straight into the meeting that had been going on for a while and was caught, definitely late and therefore fined. I went to my locker and threw on a T-shirt and my football pants and waited. About that time, the team meeting broke up and guys began to filter out, heading toward the defensive room.

Smelling like smoke, with soot all over my face, I just walked into the defensive room as if nothing had happened and plopped down. Some of the guys were looking at me but said nothing as our coach, Ernie Stautner, began the meeting. Ernie looked at me as if he knew something was up, said nothing, and slightly grinned. I was lucky and had dodged a bullet. Apparently, someone had accidentally answered for me in the meeting roll call and Ditka had missed me not being there. The fire was out and I was not fined. What a day!

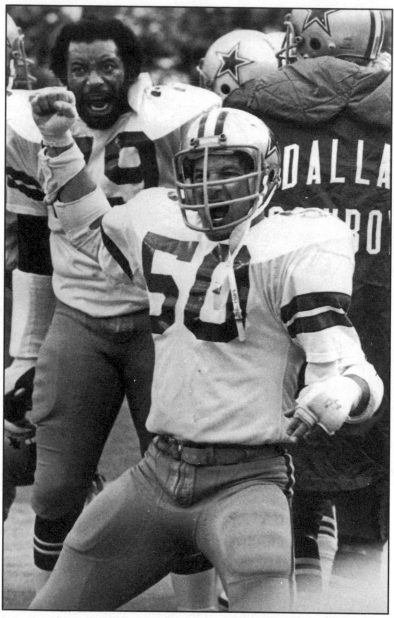

D.D. Lewis had a fly-by-the-seat-of-your-pants style in the 1970s. He purchased a lake house and we nearly burned it down one day.

Photo courtesy of www.CowboysWeekly.com

"Watch out for the..."

Charlie Waters and I rode motorcycles in the same fashion that we played football in the NFL. We put everything we had on the field. We played with passion and intensity because we loved what we were doing. We were consumed by the high our performances created. We lived and prepared exhaustively for Sundays on the turf. When we were on the field, the whole world could have been on fire and we would not have noticed. We did not want the game to end, and when it did we were still flying and it took some time to come back to earth.

On our days off and in the off-season, we rode motorcycles across varied terrain—over hills, around trees, down riverbanks, over mountains—to get back into our world of intensity. We would race with each other and take chances the same way we did on the field. Sometimes we rode with a group of guys who did not ride like we did. We enjoyed riding with other guys, but it seemed they were always trying to catch us. Except for Dave Edwards, our strong-side linebacker, who brought us into this dust-filled world, we were leading the pack. Dave always had a bigger and faster bike that he could handle masterfully.

The rest of the guys were out there to enjoy their day off, out of the city, cruising on their bikes through the countryside. Charlie and I were riding like hell to escape.

We rode our bikes in different areas, most of the time not too far from Dallas. We called one of the places Great Southwest because the trails wound around the hilly, mesquite-covered area that surrounded the retired Great Southwest Airport between Dallas and Ft. Worth. It was not too far for us to drive to ride on our days off.

It was a tricky area with winding trails. If you did not know them well and lost control, sometimes you would find yourself flying off the bluff at the very top of a hill. Riding dirt bikes was a lot like playing on Sundays. The game called for playing hard and

Riding motorcycles off-road was the way I relaxed and took my mind off football. *Photo courtesy of Cliff Harris*

pushing yourself to the edge and sometimes going wildly to the very limits of control. A push over that line could hurt you.

Bob Breunig, our middle linebacker who took charge after Lee Roy Jordan retired, rode with us one day at Great Southwest. Bob was strong and smart. He was tough and knew how to make the Flex system work for his style of play. He was not a reaction-type player, but more of an Xs-and-Os player—he filled the hole that was defined in the playbook. Landry liked that, a perfect design to fit into the middle cog of his very structured system.

Bob rode the bikes much the same way he played—straight line, fast and hard, not much curving—but he went full speed. Charlie and I had the advantage of knowing the trails because we

Bob Breunig demonstrates the latest diving technique. That had to have hurt.
Photo courtesy of www.CowboysWeekly.com

had lost ourselves at Great Southwest on quite a few weekend trips. We would take off and lose Breun-dog (as we called him) while flying through the narrow, winding trails. When the trails came out of the woods and into the flat, they straightened out. Bob would give it full throttle to the point of out of control to catch up with us just in time to see us disappear back into the woods or creek bed. One of those times, after we came out of the curvy trails, there was a straight stretch for about 300 yards.

Charlie and I knew that about two-thirds of the way down, a barbed-wire fence had been strung completely across the road. The road deceptively and dangerously continued for about 100 yards past the fence. The key was to turn right, before you hit the fence, on a path that skewed off into the woods. Charlie and I took off down the straight stretch, with Bob flying behind us at full throttle trying to catch up. About the time we turned into the woods, we first heard then saw Bob go flying straight past us. He had been to Great Southwest with us before, and we thought he remembered the fence. He obviously didn't. He quickly glanced over at us with a look of "Oh-oh!" fear on his face.

By the time we yelled for him to stop, he was already jamming on his brakes. He laid his bike down, but it was too late. We saw him sliding on the concrete, bouncing along, before he hit the fence. When he stopped, he found himself tangled in a bunch of barbed wire—helter-skelter, like Steve McQueen in *The Great Escape*. Bob, as they say in the motocross world, really "ate it." He was completely engulfed in the barbed wire, lying on the ground with his bike still whining and spinning in circles, with a wide-open throttle. We turned off his bike and unwound a bloody Bob from his snare. He was scratched up pretty good.

We told him he needed to ride more under control…

 ## Whittling
By Walt Garrison

I started whittling in training camp my second year because I needed something to do. There were morning and afternoon practices. In between, there were two or three hours of idle time.

Most people slept. I couldn't sleep. I still can't sleep. So I went down to the local hardware store and bought a whittling block, a pocketknife and a piece of wood. I sharpened the knife and sat there and began whittling. I started out whittling simple things such as chains, balls, and boxes. Then I got more advanced. It was therapeutic for me.

Walt Garrison (32) was already a seasoned vet when I joined the team, but we quickly became friends. He roomed with Charlie Waters.

Photo courtesy of www.CowboysWeekly.com

I have a picture of a bunch of us whittling the following year in training camp. I really started out of boredom, but then I couldn't quit. I did it during the season, too.

I was on a road trip and was whittling in the hotel the night before a game. I cut my finger and the bone was sticking out. Charlie Waters, who was my roommate, freaked out and said, "You are going to bleed to death!"

I told Charlie to call the team's orthopedic surgeon, Marvin Knight, but he was out, so I told him to run down to the trainer's to get some gauze, and I cut myself a couple of butterflies. He got me a bucket of ice. I put my finger in it and fell asleep. Charlie stayed up all night. He really thought I was going to die.

So, the next day, I went to the game early and showed Dr. Knight my finger. He put 19 stitches in it, so it would hold. He gave me some novocaine and warned me, "Don't tell Coach Landry."

Believe it or not, I actually caught a touchdown pass in that game and Coach Landry was none the wiser.

Super Teams

Hawaii was the perfect setting for the Super Teams competition after a long wearisome year in pro football. It was warm and sunny, a beach getaway in February from cold Dallas. The Super Teams were composed of guys from the teams that played in the NFL's Super Bowl—the Pittsburgh Steelers and my Dallas Cowboys—and MLB's World Series. The games took place soon after the NFL Pro Bowl. Ten of the more popular or "name" guys were also invited to attend. Though it took place in a relaxing environment, you were still competing against the talented (but relaxed) baseball players from the

World Series and the guys we had just faced in the Super Bowl. We did not want to lose anything to either of those groups of guys.

The competition was in areas different than our sports. The events were made up primarily as relays. There was a swimming relay with four guys swimming 50-meter legs and a medley running relay comprised of two 110-yard legs, one 220 and one killer 440-yard leg. Charlie and I were in a team tandem bicycle race with three other pairs of players. There was a fun, 10-guy outrigger canoe race in the lagoon next to the Waimea Hilton where Ralph Neely fell out of our boat into the lagoon. During beach volleyball, the coordinated baseball guys out-teamed the clumsy football giants. There was also an obstacle course relay race, where pairs of guys raced against each other scrambling over a 15-foot wall—some couldn't make it—across the monkey bars, over some hurdles and then running 20 yards to the finish. The competition climaxed with a grueling beach tug-o-war. We set a painful one hour, 15 minute record and won in the hot sand. All the racing events were based on the cumulative scores of the participants. So if one guy did poorly, the team lost. The spotlight was really on the individual performances in each of the competitions.

The guys at Super Teams were not only great athletes in their sports, but by nature were very competitive. We all wanted to win for different reasons. We certainly did not want to get beat in anything by the smaller and quicker baseball players. And particularly as Cowboys, we wanted to show the world we were better athletes than those nasty Steelers, even though they had just beaten us in the Super Bowl. We had revenge on our minds. Also, to add even more pressure, the competition was a widely watched, nationally televised event. If you were beaten individually, you were isolated and would be embarrassed in front of a large audience that could actually see your face, unlike football.

Lynn Swann had a star performance against us in the Super Bowl. I had a verbal battle with him in the press, which heightened both of our exposure levels. The routes he ran in the Super Bowl did not give me a chance to really give him a shot, which was, I think, by design. He was the guy I had to compete against in all the individual competitions. I really wanted to beat him. Though I did not necessarily want to be paired against him, it seemed like on all the competitions we ended up facing each other. I knew he was a great athlete from USC. All I could do was give it all I had.

The first competition that paired me against Swanny was the obstacle course. It was a critical time in the competition, because after all of the previous events, our teams were tied. The obstacle course would put one team ahead. Charlie and four of our other guys had already competed against their counterparts. Robert Newhouse was next. He ran against Jack Hamm, and Jack was given a penalty for knocking over a hurdle, making our accumulated time one second ahead of the Steelers. It was up to Swann. He had to beat me by more than a second for them to win the event. Everyone was betting on the great athlete, Swann, to beat me.

I thought, "There is no way he will beat me!"

Charlie came up and gave me an unnecessary pep talk while I was standing facing the wall with Lynn lined up beside me. Knowing Swan had to beat me by a full second to win, I wasn't going to let that happen. My goal was to push Swan hard and force him into making a mistake and drawing a penalty, without making a mistake myself.

We took off and both scaled the 15-foot wall as if it were not even there. We zipped through the monkey bars side by side. We raced through the entire obstacle course running parallel. Neither ever took the lead. We flew over the hurdles, both leaping over the water obstacle and crossed the finish line dead even. Swann and I

...ad Fu Manchu facial hair and I swear he had hair implants ...brows to form an upside down "V" above each eye. He ...d a disgusted look on his face. I'm surprised he didn't get ...n implants on each side of his forehead.

...e year, on our first night at the Pro Bowl, several of us met ...tails at the hotel bar in San Diego. Behind the bar, there was ... aquarium. It was every bit as wide as the bar and stretched ...loor to ceiling. There was no telling how many gallons of ...it held. It made up the entire wall behind the bar. It was the ..."signature."

...Cliff and I met the three bad-boy linemen from the Cardinals ...peace-making cocktail and to share some war stories.

...Conrad had already been entertaining himself with a couple ...shots of tequila prior to us joining them. The five of us sitting ...und the table like we were all teammates was an unlikely ...enario.

I don't remember when Conrad slipped out, but I know when ...e rejoined us. Sitting there, swapping lies and sharing libation with ...my new friends, I glanced over at the bar, and at that very instant, a large whale-like figure plunged into the water.

The bright, tropical fish scattered as the mammoth figure flailed away. Water and fish were displaced and landed on the bar.

"Look!" I exclaimed, pointing at the tank. There was Conrad, in all his glory, swimming around with the fish. Thank goodness he kept his boxers shorts on. He managed to swim to the glass wall overlooking us and pressed his evil face up against the glass, eyes wide open. When the bartender wheeled around he almost fell down from shock.

It took a while for the police to retrieve the massive man. Amazingly, after some autographs, Conrad charmed both the police and the hotel managers into writing it off as just a little fun dip.

What a character. Conrad Dobler's reputation remained intact.

Hawaii was a beautiful backdrop for our "friendly" competition against other players in the NFL and Major League Baseball. *Photo courtesy of Cliff Harris*

tied; therefore, with the Cowboys' one-second edge, we won the event. Man, I was happy the team won, and I did what I needed to do for the team, but I did not beat him individually. The real test was coming up, though: the medley relay.

The next-to-last event was the medley relay. When we arrived in Hawaii the first day, they brought us all together to watch a video of a previous year's event. It featured the Vikings vs. the Dolphins who had been in SB VIII. In the medley relay, Paul Krause, the Vikes' Hall of Fame free safety, was running the 440-yard anchor leg. His teammates beat their guys and gave Krause a 30-yard head start over Dolphins Hall of Fame receiver Paul Warfield. When Warfield got the baton, he really took off. We watched him close the gap on

Krause. He passed Krause with about 10 yards left in the race and won. Krause, I am sure, was embarrassed. After watching that tape, no one wanted to run the 440.

When we all got together to determine who would run what leg, I was a little nervous. My teammates knew I ran track at Ouachita Baptist and ran the 440. It was a tough race—full speed around the whole track. I argued in vain that I should run one of the sprint legs. I knew there really was no one else who could run the 440 better than I could. I did not like it. Guess who was running the 440 for the Steelers…right, Lynn Swann!

Man, I did not sleep the night before the race. I knew Swann had speed, but I wasn't sure about his toughness—which the 440 demanded. I certainly did not want what happened to Krause to happen to me. Preston Pearson believed he could beat Rocky Bleier. Robert Newhouse was running, and he could beat L.C. Greenwood. Then, handing off to me was speedy receiver Golden Richards, who they all but guaranteed would beat Mel Blount by at least 10 or 15 yards in his 220-yard race, giving me a comfortable lead.

The race did not go as planned. The gun went off, and my heart was in my stomach. I was watching our guys run and hand off. Newhouse handed the baton to Golden with a 10-yard head start over Mel. I saw it and was happy. Then Blount, who is 6 feet 4 inches began to really take off. He caught Golden in the turn and began to pass him. The officials moved me from the inside position on the track to the outside position—lining up Swann on the inside. Golden sped up right at the end, and Swann and I took our handoffs simultaneously.

It was me against him, head to head, man against man—just the way I expected. There was no way I was going to let a guy who beat us in the Super Bowl beat me in this 440. I would have died first. We took off and headed for the curve. I really sprinted, beat Swann to the curve, and was running in front of him. I put

everything I had into the race on t[...] my heels. I poured on more steam a[...] yards left, the Hall of Famer was be[...] finished and the timers told me I ran[...] thought, but I know I could have run e[...] beat Lynn Swann and the Steelers. I was[...]

41 The Devil Made M[...]
By Charlie Waters

Cardinals guard Conrad Dobler was out[...] himself in the NFL—and he did. He wasn't satis[...] as the good player he was; he insisted on bein[...] player. Dirty is a mild description, he was more li[...] he would pinch, gouge, bite, and kick. Sometimes [...] in his socks and gouge us with it. These crude shena[...] occasional, but on every play. He was mischievous to[...]

Our rivalry with the then-St. Louis Cardinals was[...] sprinkled with color and excitement. Jim Hart, the gre[...] Cardiac Cardinals, was surrounded by some quality s[...] speedy wide receiver Mel Gray, Hall of Fame tight end Jac[...] and running backs Jim Otis and Terry Metcalf. But t[...] strength was in their offensive line: tackle Dan Dierdorf, cen[...] Banks, and Conrad Dobler. All three were Pro Bowlers.

Conrad, though nasty, was really a fun guy to be around. H[...] one of the opponents that you hated, because he was always causi[...] problem for you; if he was your teammate, though, you'd love him[...] don't think he was mean by nature; he developed it. He re-invente[...] himself. He was a true character and thrived on attention. He got that[...] attention by acting devilish on the field and off. In public he[...] complemented his bad actions with his mean, disgruntled looks.

St. Louis Cardinals offensive lineman Conrad Dobler was a wild man—on *and* off the field! *Photo courtesy of www.CowboysWeekly.com*

On the Hook

A friend of mine in the oil business, Curtis Leggett, had a ranch in the piney woods of East Texas. There was a little lake on the ranch loaded with big bass. Though the lake was small, the bass were lunkers.

Randy White escaped his ferocious football world by fishing. Randy, along with Ed Jones and Harvey Martin, created havoc as pass rushers on opposing QBs as the Doomsday II defense. They made my job easier. Randy fished the same way he rushed the passer—with passion and intensity.

Early one summer morning, Randy and I took off from my house in North Dallas headed to East Texas for some fishing. Another buddy, Mike Jaccar, was tagging along, more to visit than to fish. In college, stocky Mike played point guard for Southern Methodist University. Mike worked with me at Max Williams' US Companies. He was a fun guy to hang out with, but not really a fisherman.

We reached Curtis' place early and started fishing. We used a 12-foot, flat-bottom boat with three seats and a trolling motor in the front. I relinquished the prime front seat to Randy so he could drive and have the best chance to catch fish. Sitting in the front seat of the boat meant you controlled the direction with the motor and, more importantly, could cast your bait into the prime spot first. Fish generally hit the first cast, not the second.

I was in the second-best spot in the very back, so I could also hit some good spots. Mike was along more for the camaraderie and sat in the middle seat. He had to watch where Randy and I cast and threw his lure elsewhere—definitely not the best spot.

Randy and I were casting and working our top-water baits with precision and skill, using action—jerking movements—to entice the big bass lurking below the lily pads to come up and hit. Mike, on the other hand, was fishing machine-gun fashion. He would cast out his

Imagine having this brute—Randy White—at the end of your fishing line!

Photo by Russ Russell, courtesy of www.CowboysWeekly.com

bait and reel it back in very quickly, with no action, and then cast again. I told him to slow down and work the bait and he would have a better chance of catching a big one. He slowed down some, but he was not very patient, and before long he was casting and reeling fast again.

Mike also had to be careful to only cast out the sides, perpendicular to the boat. If he cast anywhere else, there was the danger of hooking Randy or me. I had to remind Mike of that several times while dodging his lure.

Mike was an excitable guy with a lot of energy. On one quick cast, he lost his focus as he was aiming past me in the back. When he took his rod back and started forward on his cast, his rod suddenly jerked to a stop. On his wind-up, Mike whizzed the line backwards and the hooks of his lure lodged into the middle of Randy's back.

Randy, who was facing the front of the boat with his back to Mike, jerked straight up and grunted "Ugh!" That was it. Mike's lure was stick bait with three treble hooks. Two of the three sets were stuck deep into Randy's bleeding back.

Mike was facing me, frozen with a look of dread, and he told me, "I hooked Randy White in the back with my bait!"

"Jake," I said, using his nickname, "you are on your own!"

Randy, looking straight ahead, calmly asked, "Could you get the hooks out of my back?"

Mike eagerly spun around towards Randy and said, "Sure!"

He took out a pair of pliers and wiggled those bloody hooks out of Randy's hide.

Randy never turned around. He said, "That all right. It's getting me ready for training camp!" Randy is one tough customer.

I am sure Mike's life flashed before his eyes when it happened. We fished the rest of the day and landed some big ones, but none bigger than the one Mike snagged. Randy had an especially good training camp that year…thanks to Mike Jaccar!

French Quarter Madness

Charlie Waters and I decided one night after practice before the Super Bowl we needed a little excitement, so we made the 20-minute trip into the French Quarter from our Holiday Inn in Metairie. As soon as our evening meeting session ended, we grabbed a cab and headed into the city. We asked the cab driver to take us to Bourbon Street because that was the only street name we knew.

When we arrived in the French Quarter, we could not believe what we saw. We had never seen this other side of the Super Bowl. Although there were some people dressed in silver and blue, the streets were mainly jammed with orange and blue. People were disguised as Orange Crush cans. Others were either dressed or painted half in orange, half in blue. The Broncos fans were rowdy and rambunctious—a fun-loving group—celebrating the success their team had had for the first time.

After we had been walking around for a while looking at all the French Quarter goings-on, Charlie and I decided to visit the bar, Pat O'Brien's, to have a world-famous Hurricane. We wandered around for a bit before stumbling into the crowded and loud bar. At first we blended right in and tried to remain incognito. We agreed to just have one drink and then head out. We ordered, sat back, and began to take in the character of the place. We felt comfortable that we could go unnoticed because we looked just like normal guys having a drink at the bar. We were not giants like Ed "Too Tall" Jones or as visible as Roger Staubach.

Our anonymity was short-lived. Before we had half-finished our drinks, a Cowboys fan at the end of the bar looked up and screamed at the top of his voice, "There are Cliff Harris and Charlie Waters!"

It seemed like everyone turned to look. Of course, the bar was filled with football fans so they immediately started moving our way.

Before we knew it, we were surrounded with people wanting autographs and talking about the game.

I started feeling claustrophobic and wanted out. So did Charlie. We had wanted some excitement, but not this much. About that time, some Broncos fan yelled, "Cowboys suck!" I knew we were in trouble. More Broncos fans joined in the heckling, but I didn't care what they were saying; I just wanted to escape. Trouble was brewing.

I said to Charlie, "Let's get out of here!" He said, "Right!" and we began to push our way through the drunken crowd. We weren't making much headway, and then the trouble came to a head and it was too late.

Two rival fans began to fight—defending us, or something equally ridiculous. They were knocking chairs over as they battered each other. We ducked and pushed our way to the door as the fight intensified and more and more crazed fans got involved. We tried to stay out of the way but some guys started pushing us. Our adrenaline kicked in and we started to get mad. We decided it was now or never—either get out of the bar or get into some major trouble.

I said, "Follow me." I ducked my head and pretended I was running back a kickoff through the crowd. We bumped a few people on the way out, but made it. We ran down the street and hailed a cab. We high-tailed it back to our safe haven at the Holiday Inn.

During the cab ride we breathed a sigh of relief and decided that playing in the Super Bowl would be enough excitement for us.

    ## Skoal Man
By Walt Garrison

In the early 1970s, NFL Films did a film called *The Hunter*, which was about three professional football players who had weird off-season occupations or hobbies.

Carl Eller of the Minnesota Vikings was trying to become an actor. He was going to acting school. Later he was in a couple of films and an episode of the TV show *The Fall Guy.* Ben Davidson of the Oakland Raiders drove motorcycles. He wasn't even into racing, but he liked topography. He would get a map, start off riding in California and wind up in Montana.

I was into rodeo.

So the film crew came to Mineral Wells, Texas, to tape a rodeo segment with me. I also was doing snuff. And they talked about the snuff and rodeo on the segment, which was shown on national television. An advertising executive in New York City happened to see the segment.

U.S. Smokeless Tobacco had never aired a television commercial, and the company asked me if I would be the spokesman on a commercial. I thought I needed to tell somebody at the Cowboys before I accepted. I asked Al Ward, who was then the Cowboys assistant general manager and he said the Cowboys "believe it would be bad for your image." I told U.S. Smokeless Tobacco I couldn't do the commercial.

But they could never find anybody to do it. So they came back to me a year later and offered me more money to appear on the commercial. It was definitely more money than I was making playing football. I went to Al and told him they had called again. And he repeated that the club believed it was bad for my image.

I said, "This is my image. And you all have made it that way. All you ever talk about in regards to me is the rodeo, dippin' snuff, blue jeans, and boots. You have made the image what it is."

I asked if there was any legal reason why I couldn't do it. He said no, so I told him I was going to appear on the commercial. I became their spokesman over the years, and it was probably the best move I ever made. My log house is the house that snuff built. Playing football damn sure didn't build my house.

Walt Garrison (32) was a spokesman for U.S. Smokeless Tobacco—the makers of Skoal—for many years, despite the Cowboys' warning that it was bad for his image. *Photo courtesy of www.CowboysWeekly.com*

Just a Small Dent

In the off-season of my ninth year, I was surprised to receive a call from Ouachita alum Bob Walker. He was ahead of me in school, and though I did not know Bob very well, I always liked him. He played on the OBU basketball team and was a mild-mannered guy and a good athlete. He told me his family owned Eldocraft Boat Company and he had a "deal" just for me. He wanted me to promote a boat for them; it was going to be called the "Cliff Harris Special" fishing boat.

I was familiar with Eldocraft boats and thought they had a good reputation. He went on to tell me he wanted me to come to Arkansas, take some pictures with the boat, and then he would give it to me.

I was expecting an aluminum flat-bottom boat with a small motor and thought, "What the heck! I'll do it." I knew that July was the end of my summer and a very busy time of lifting and conditioning before the start of training camp, so I thought it might be tough for me to pull the trip off. But I told him I would do it if it could be done in June on Lake Degray near Arkadelphia.

I thought I could kill two birds with one stone: get the boat and visit my folks in Hot Springs, which was very near there. He quickly agreed and we picked a date in June, which was only about a month away.

June arrived quickly, and before I knew it, I was to meet Bob at the Lake Degray Lodge and the photo shoot was scheduled for right after lunch.

The only problem was that I didn't have a truck or a trailer hitch to pull the boat back to Dallas…but I knew Charlie did.

I met him in the training room and asked if I could borrow his truck for the day. I would drive up to Arkadelphia in the morning and bring it back that night. He had a brand-new SUV, but being the trusting buddy that he was, he agreed to let me borrow it anyway.

As I was leaving the training facility with his keys, he only had one request. He looked into my eyes and said, "Cliff, don't wreck it, okay?"

"No problem!" I said. "See you later."

A friend of mine from Dallas came along. She lived at home with her mom and had to be back that night anyway, so the plan was perfect.

Off we went, and after about five hours we arrived in Arkadelphia and the lodge at the edge of the lake. We went inside and found Bob. I asked him where the boat was. He said it was in the parking lot. I went outside and looked around. I saw a boat, but thought, "That can't be my boat…it is too awesome!" But it was my boat, and it definitely was not what I expected. It was blue and silver fiberglass—an 18-footer with a 150 HP Merc and a trolling motor in front. I thought, "This is cool!" I was very excited to do the shoot, so we all headed to the lake with the boat.

It was a hot day and we shot pictures from different locations on the lake. It took several hours, and by the end of the day I was exhausted and so was my friend. We had a long drive ahead, so we decided to skip the visit to my parents. It was dusk when we said goodbye to Bob, hooked the boat up, got something to eat, and took off for Dallas.

After a couple of hours my eyes were heavy and I was getting very sleepy. I told my friend, "I just need to take a short cat nap. All I need are 20 minutes." She was reluctant, having never towed a boat before. I convinced her it would be no problem.

My friend was petite, she pulled the seat up all the way. With some trepidation, she took off down the road. She wasn't behind the wheel for very long before I fell right asleep with my head against the window. Suddenly, I awoke to my head being banged against the window. Confused and disoriented, I looked over and saw a look of panic over her face. Her hands on the steering wheel were being yanked from one side to the other. I looked back and the boat was doing the same, swinging wildly from one side of the truck to the other. The truck was weaving back and forth across the interstate. I reached over with one hand and grabbed the steering wheel, trying to stop its movement, but it was too late. The boat swung around and crashed into the side of Charlie's new truck with a horrific bang. I managed to steer the truck to the side of the road and out of the way of the semi-trucks that were screaming past.

When we came to a stop, my friend was balling. I ask her what happened and she explained how she reached up to adjust the mirror and accidentally moved the wheel to the right. Then she overcorrected, which started the boat trailer fishtailing. The whole incident had taken only a few seconds and it had happened right after I had dozed off.

There was nothing we could do, stuck in the middle of Nowhere, Texas, two hours from Dallas, but wait for help. I told her, "Don't worry. Everything will be fine," But I didn't believe it myself.

Semis were flying by, but no one stopped. After we had been there 30 minutes or so, pondering what to do, a truck pulled up in front of us. A guy got out and knocked on my window.

"Hey, you guys need some help?" he asked. "I'm with Handy Dan's Interstate Repair."

I said, "Heck yes, we do."

He opened the back of his truck and it lit up like a flying saucer. It lit up the whole countryside. The truck was full of tools. He pulled out a welding torch and went to work on my trailer hitch, which was bent at a 90-degree angle. After about 30 minutes he had straightened the hitch and we were headed back down the road. Everything was fine…except for the major dent in Charlie's truck.

We arrived in Dallas very late and I took my friend home. The next morning I dreaded what was ahead of me—telling Charlie. I knew he would be hopping mad, so I attempted to soften the blow by taking his truck to be washed and waxed. I drove over to the practice field where he was working out and found him doing flyes

My Eldocraft boat—the Cliff Harris Special—was speedy and maneuverable, just like me! *Photo courtesy of Cliff Harris*

on a weight machine. I stood in front of him, face to face. All I said was "Charlie," and he knew.

With an eerie calm, he said, "You wrecked my truck."

"Come outside and look. It's not bad," I reassured him.

He got up and we walked out. I had parked his truck so he would see the polished, undamaged side first. He took a few steps around the truck and said, "Oh," like he had known I would wreck the truck, but thought the damage would be worse.

Of course, I had his truck repaired, but after that incident, I found it hard to borrow vehicles. I guess word really does travel fast.

CHAPTER SIX

RETIREMENT AND BEYOND

Making the Decision

Pro football players exist in a physical world that never changes. The ages of the individuals never vary, only the faces change. Everyone seems to always be in their twenties. Time stops in that exciting, but critical, moment of life right after college graduation. The only way players sense they are growing old is when they find themselves spending more time in the whirlpool with nagging injuries. If players are not careful they can start to feel invincible and want to play forever.

It was a tough decision to announce my retirement, earlier than everyone expected, from football in April 1980. Our spring off-season conditioning program was to start with a meeting that Monday. I had never missed any of those sessions, but I knew it would be pointless to start the program and then retire. Roger Staubach had told me he was planning to announce his retirement that same Monday, and everyone knew it. I called him at home and told him I did not want to upstage him, which would have been impossible anyway, but I was going to make my announcement the Friday before the training program started. He was shocked and asked me if I was sure, and I said yes. I knew it was time to let it go.

Even though my neck was bothering me, I could have played a few more years. I would have had to change my game, though, and I did not like those prospects. I enjoyed going full speed and hitting and committing 100 percent. I did not want to have to manipulate any part of my game just to hang on.

At the time I was working with an oil exploration company started by Max Williams, a former Southern Methodist University basketball star. Max was a great guy who understood athletes and also was a very successful businessman. I was really enjoying working with Max and the booming oil business. I was making more money (with less pain) than I had been with the Cowboys. I also had deferred some of my income from the Cowboys and could invest it in the oil business.

Although it was productive—we barely lost the NFC divisional playoff to Los Angeles—my last year with Cowboys was not fun. Charlie Waters tore up his knee in the preseason and was out for the whole year. His presence always made my job easier and more fun, because he made me a better player with our teamwork approach to the game. His theory of the game was sometimes different than mine, but he brought a different perspective that I later embraced, which helped make us more successful. He was often right, although I would seldom admit it. We really worked together exceptionally well, read each other's minds, and worked hard to keep opposing quarterbacks guessing at what the heck we were doing.

Also that season, Thomas "Hollywood" Henderson had been playing strong-side linebacker, and although he was a great athlete, he was a real pain. He sometimes made big plays, but his mistakes had to be fixed by other players. He rarely knew the game plan or what to do because he slept through our meetings. Charlie had more patience with him than I did and would tell him what to do in practice and the game. When Hollywood asked me, I would tell him to stay awake and learn it himself.

All of these factors combined to tell me it was time to quit, so I did.

I think my early retirement was a shock to most. Because of my passion for, commitment to, and enjoyment of the game, most thought they would have to drag me off the field. I liked to keep people guessing—from quarterbacks on the field to the pro football experts—and that's why I quit when I did. I never wanted anyone to think they had me figured out.

After the announcement I flew to Salt Lake City, went skiing, and forgot about football.

Well, as much as I could.

My instincts kept bothering me, telling me to go back. I think Coach Landry also thought I was coming back. I knew Charlie had worked hard and rehabilitated his injured knee, and Randy Hughes could work into my spot, but when July came around, I was hurting because I knew the guys were heading to Thousand Oaks. Strange as it may sound, I enjoyed training camp and really wanted to go, but held off and submersed myself in the oil business even more.

The summer went by fast, and I followed the team in the paper. Then the preseason games began, and I got antsy. The Cowboys returned to Dallas to play a preseason game against the Houston Oilers.

The year before, we played the Oilers in the Astrodome during the preseason. Charlie had already hurt his knee and Randy Hughes could not play because he had suddenly "pulled" a muscle. I had to play most of the game on the old, rough Astrodome turf, and lined up against the toughest running back I ever faced, Oilers running back Earl Campbell.

He had a field day.

The Oilers used two tight ends and ran Earl up the middle. There were gaping holes because the rookie defensive linemen could not figure out how to close the gaps. I ended up meeting Earl (who had a running start at me) head to head all day. At the end of the game I was worn out, with all of the skin worn off my elbows and knees from banging into Earl full speed. It was not fun!

A year later, on the night of the 1980 preseason game, I went for the first time to Clayton Williams' ranch party, which he threw at the end of every summer. Tom Kelly, a friend of mine from Midland, Texas, who was just starting his very successful oil business, came with me. There were about 2,000 people scattered all over Clayton's West Texas ranch, complete with a boot-shaped swimming pool with an Aggie emblem in the bottom.

Tom and I were sitting on the side of a hill, listening to Merle Haggard on the stage below, but I still felt I wanted to be a Cowboy, and I told Tom that. I will never forget his response.

"Cliff, just think, you could be in Texas Stadium where it is 120 degrees, trying to tackle Earl Campbell. Instead you are sitting here on the side of a hill, and it's 75 degrees, drinking a beer with a good-looking girl and me by your side. Your future is here, not there."

I knew he was right, and from that point on, I moved out of football and on with life.

Facing Landry

The Cowboys had a successful preseason in 1980, but before they finished, I received an unexpected call. I was at home when the phone rang, and when I answered it, I thought it might be a prank call when the caller said, "This is Coach Landry, and I would like to visit with you."

I started to say, "Who is this really?" But I caught myself.

"Hello, Coach."

"Can you come by my house? I would like to talk to you as soon as possible."

"I can come tomorrow evening."

"That's fine. See you then."

My head started spinning as I hung up the phone. I wasn't sure why he wanted to see me. I had overcome all of the pressure points that challenged me about my decision to call it quits, but I knew Coach had a very persuasive way about him. I thought this might be another test for me.

Coach Landry and his wife, Alicia, lived in a really cool house in the Bluffview area. Their house actually hung on the edge of the "bluff" on a short, dead-end street discreetly hidden in middle of Dallas.

The next day I rang his doorbell and Mrs. Landry answered the door. She was a beautiful woman with a lot of grace and poise. She asked me to come in.

"Tommy, Cliff is here," she called.

"Wow," I thought, "she calls him Tommy!"

Coach came walking up in his stately style from another level in his house. Like my house, all the back of his was completely glass and looked out over the trees. We walked down a level into his office.

He and I were standing looking into his backyard and the bluff below. His office was filled with trophies and memorabilia from his days with the Cowboys, with the Giants, and at the University of Texas. Pictures of Lombardi. Man, was I impressed.

"Go on ahead and sit down," he said, gesturing to the couch.

He sat down beside me.

"Cliff," he said immediately, "I do not want to pressure you, but I would like for you to come back this year and play. I know you can do it."

The statement floored me. It was the first time I had ever been in his house, and I was a bit nervous and definitely felt his pressure. I summoned up my courage.

"Coach, my future is not in football now," I explained. "It is in the oil business."

"I understand," he paused and continued to surprise me. "You know, I am not sure if Charlie's knee will hold up all season. Will you come back if he goes down?"

"Definitely," I said without hesitation. "You can count on me."

"Will you stay in shape?"

"Yes," I promised.

I knew this was the point in preseason he had to make difficult strategic decisions on players and positions—who to keep and who to cut—because the season was about to begin. If I had said I would not come back, then he would have had to keep more defensive backs. My promise gave him some flexibility.

As I walked out of Coach Landry's house, I breathed a sigh of relief and felt like I had made it. I had stayed away through all of the tough parts—training camp, preseason, and Coach Landry. I was committed now to the real world. Things were going to be great.

That is, until the mid-1980s when the oil, banking, and real estate markets crashed in Dallas. Then I wanted the security of pro football back.

12 Don't Blame Jackie
By Roger Staubach

When I look back on my football career, there are two really big games that meant a lot to me. One was at Navy when we were the No. 2 team in the country. We played Texas for the national championship in January of 1964. And the second, of course, was when we had a chance to win our third Super Bowl against Pittsburgh in Super Bowl XIII. The common denominator was that we played two really great teams—Texas was the No. 1 college team in the country; and that Pittsburgh team was one of the greatest teams that ever played in the NFL—and they both had great defenses.

In fact, we lost the Texas game 28-6. We could not run the football; they totally shut us down. We did have a good passing game and were very effective throwing the football, yet I was being chased all over the field. That's probably the sorest I've ever been after a football game. Their defense just went after me. It was a tough game and a tough loss to a great football team. Defensively they were unbelievable.

The 1977 Cowboys were probably as good as we've ever been— maybe one of the best teams ever. We had a stellar offense and a fantastic defense, but we happened to be playing the Pittsburgh Steelers. What took place in the game was this: If there are four or five plays that don't go your way you don't complain about it, but when you're playing against a great team like the Steelers, you've got to get your share of those plays; and we did not.

The unfortunate thing is that the play most people felt made a difference in the game really wasn't the difference. There are a number of plays that led to the loss—there was an interception I threw before the half, we had a fumble on a kickoff, we had a whining call against a referee, there was a horrible interference call. But my third-quarter pass to Jackie Smith was the most controversial play because we lost the game by four points. People blame Jackie, which I think is one of the most unfair things I have observed in my athletic life. He didn't deserve it. Giving the Steelers all the credit due, we needed to make sure we didn't make mistakes, but we did. Of course, Pittsburgh caused some of those mistakes.

Losing Super Bowl XIII to the Pittsburgh Steelers still haunts many of the Cowboys who played in it. *Photo courtesy of www.CowboysWeekly.com*

The play that Jackie was involved in was a goal-line play in the third quarter. It was designed so that Jackie would run to the back of the end zone and hook. He was a safety valve. We're in a third-and-one on the 11-yard line and Coach Landry by mistake sends in the wrong play, plus we had three tight ends that came in for that play and it was strictly practice for the goal line. They were sent in on the 11 and they were all coming in the huddle. I had to call time out. I went off the field and said, "Hey, Coach, this is a goal-line play." But the players were already in the game and they had to stay in. So we said run it like a goal-line play, which makes sense, because goal-line and short-yardage defenses are similar. It's just that when you're on the goal line you have the protection of the back of the end zone if you're on defense, yet they are still similar defenses.

Sure enough, I went in the huddle and said, "Hey listen, let's run this like we set it up in practice and run it as a goal-line play." Jackie was a safety valve so he always practiced running to the back of the end zone, which was 11 or 12 yards. Now we're on the 11-yard line, and it turns out that he is the primary receiver, everybody else was covered. He's running 21 yards now, but he's running to the back of the end zone and it took him longer. If he would have stopped at the goal line, that would have been the same as the way we practiced it, but he ran it like a goal-line play. He starts to turn around and I threw the ball early. It was not a good pass, it was low and obviously he didn't expect it. As he turned around, I think it was a shock that the ball was there and he wasn't able to make the catch. Again, I released it quickly and it wasn't a good pass, but we kicked a field goal and the score was 21-17 in the third quarter.

It's just unbelievable that Jackie was blamed for a solid team beating us 35-31. There were a number of errors that were more costly in that game than that particular play. Ironically, the play was the wrong play. It shouldn't have been called, and Jackie should not have been the scapegoat for losing to a great Steelers football team.

Ring of Honor

Since 1991, I've held a charity golf tournament in Dallas. The money we raised for many years went to help abused kids through the Court Appointed Special Advocate (CASA) program, and now it helps the American Diabetes Association fight for those who suffer with the terrible disease of diabetes. Charlie has co-sponsored the tournament with me many of those years. Though it is a worthy event, it's also very demanding of our time and energy. A banquet kicks off the event, but the crescendo is the golf tournament held the next morning. Every year, a bunch of our former football buddies and other celebrities turn out to play golf with us and raise money for a good cause. The morning of the tournament is, without exception, stressful for me.

About tee time during the 2004 tournament, all of the 60 or so teams were lined up, ready to hit the course and, in the midst of all the madness, I received a call on my cell phone. The caller said, "This is Marilyn in Jerry Jones' office. Do you have a moment to speak with Mr. Jones?"

For a split-second I thought it might be a prank call, but I hesitated to hang up because I thought I recognized Marilyn's voice. The golfers were waiting for me to say, "Go!" but I held. Jerry came on and said, "Cliff, I was calling you to see if you would be receptive to allowing the Dallas Cowboys to put your name in the Ring of Honor at Texas Stadium."

I was dumbstruck for a second. Jerry asked, "Cliff, are you still there?" I gathered myself and said, "Yes, I'm here, and Jerry, of course I would be honored to have my name in Texas Stadium."

I was thrilled and honored to be inducted into the Cowboys Ring of Honor in 2004. *Photo by AP/WWP*

After the call with Jerry ended, my thoughts went back to a time in Hot Springs, Arkansas, to a grass field at Southwest Junior High. I was in the ninth grade and out for football for the first time. I was laying face down in the grass; my head was spinning and I could not get up. I had put all of my 110 pounds of force into tackling the Vikings' starting fullback. We collided, he rang my bell and knocked the wind out of me, then kept going. As I lay there, I thought, "I'll get him next time."

I heard distant voices saying, "I think he is knocked out," and "He is too small to play football!" That upset me very much. I couldn't wait to prove them wrong. I never wanted to quit, it just made me want to get better and prove myself. I've carried that attitude with me through every phase of football and life.

I finally did prove them wrong. It took some time—about 30 years—but I did.

My mind returned to the business at hand, and we carried on with the tournament.

Before I knew it, I was riding around inside Texas Stadium on the back of a shiny new convertible. All the great Cowboys stars were in cars in front of me. Rayfield Wright and I were on our way to be inducted into the exclusive Dallas Cowboys Ring of Honor.

Everyone is gifted in some way. The success in athletics and life start first with God-given ability. In the early years in athletics there is not much difference between the best and the worst. In time, as natural growth and development occur, the gap dramatically widens. To reach the level of the pros, natural gifts are a must. The difference between the top performers, though, lies in the heart of the man.

To be honored, as I was in the Ring of Honor, also takes being ready when you happen to be in the right place at the right time. I was fortunate to have been surrounded with great players and exceptional coaches like Tom Landry and Gene Stallings. They built a system, and my style and ability fit perfectly within that system, which allowed me to excel. Many talented players take for granted their environment, their system, their coaches and teammates. Many think they do it all themselves. Then there are others in the league who, even though they may have the talent and desire, never have a chance to perform at their best because the framework in which they exist does not allow them to maximize their potential as the Landry system did for me.

I will always be grateful that I was blessed to be surrounded with such a great group of classy and talented men such as my teammates, coaches, and the Dallas Cowboys organization.

Reflections

When I am sitting and relaxing, idle thoughts come to my mind. I sometimes reflect on my life, my career, and destiny—the minuscule chance that a kid from Ouachita had of playing for the Dallas Cowboys, but then ultimately playing in five Super Bowls. Sometimes my thoughts carry me to the circumstances that led to one particular loss: Super Bowl XIII. I think, after all that happened, about how humorous it is that fate played such a fickle hand in both instances.

For me to make the team, God had to be chuckling when he aligned the stars. Of course, my preparation for that moment and being in the right place at the right time was helpful. I was fortunate to have stayed healthy and a very good understanding of football allowed me to fit right into the Landry system, which happened to be designed perfectly for me.

During my decade we had so many victories in so many exciting games. The Dallas Cowboys, as America's Team, were arguably the most well-known and respected team in sports. Even with that enormous amount of exposure, recognition, and success,

Good timing and being surrounded by great teammates and coaches gave me five Super Bowl rings. *Photo courtesy of www.CowboysWeekly.com*

our loss in Super Bowl XIII still pains me. A series of fluky plays, bad calls, and untimely miscues kept the victory just out of our grasp. I can't help but wonder why.

I feel that loss ultimately changed the destiny of the Dallas Cowboys. The narrow margin unquestionably kept some deserving Cowboys out of the Pro Football Hall of Fame. It also allowed some to argue against our being considered the Team of the Decade of the '70s. For me, looking over the whole time period, there is no doubt that we were.

Time and my induction into the Cowboys Ring of Honor have helped refocus my thinking. When I consider the broad spectrum of our exciting wins and tragic losses, I am reminded of my philosophy of life: All you can do is all you can do. In life, if you prepare as much as you can, then give it all you have, you will enjoy life and won't have regrets. Let the chips fall where they may. That is all you can do. I thoroughly enjoyed every day of practice and preparation, then playing in the games.

That, to me, is what life is all about—putting all that you have into what you are doing. That is what makes life worth living. I tell myself that this is the same as performing on that great Cowboys team; I could have done no more.

The Tale Behind the Cover Photo

The photo on the cover of this book illustrates a play that led to the NFL making a rule change after it took place in Super Bowl XIII.

In our second Super Bowl against the Steelers, our defensive game plan called for me to put pressure on quarterback Terry Bradshaw right up the middle on a safety blitz. The theory was to force him to read the defense quickly and then throw an errant pass up for grabs.

In the third quarter, with the Steelers leading 21-17, my blitz play was called. I was ready. It was a pivotal time in the game. I lined up in my normal position, so I would not give the blitz away. I took off towards the line of scrimmage between Terry's "huts" and hit the timing just right. I was on my way to deck Bradshaw. Right before the moment of collision I saw tough running back Rocky Bleier rushing over to block me. Rocky was not very big, so I decided to hurdle him. I was right on Bradshaw, so he unloaded the ball deep in desperation towards the middle where I had just vacated.

Cornerback Benny Barnes was covering Lynn Swann, who was running a deep route, like a blanket. Benny was matching Swann stride for stride. Terry's hurried pass was nowhere near Swann, who was running closer to the sideline. Swann made a desperate move inside to get closer to the ball, but he tripped over Benny who was taking away his inside route. They collided and fell to the ground in a heap. The ball also fell to the ground into the middle of the field many yards away. The official closest to the ball, back judge Pat Knight, signaled "no catch." Then a penalty flag came flying from field judge Fred Swearingen, who was not really in a position to make the call. He called Benny for pass interference.

The Cowboys players and fans went crazy. Even Pete Rozelle, the commissioner of the NFL, admitted it was a horrible call. The next year, because of this play, the NFL changed the rules to say there would be no penalty for "incidental contact."

The moral of the story: If I had jumped just a little higher or sooner I would have clocked Bradshaw for a loss and we might have won the game. Once again, fate plays its fickle hand.

Celebrate the Heroes of Texas Sports
in These Other NEW and Recent Releases from Sports Publishing!

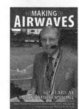